COMEBACK & BEYOND

COMEBACK & BEYOND

by
Tim Storey

Harrison House
Tulsa, OK

1st Printing, 2015

Comeback... & Beyond   Paperback Version
ISBN 978-168031-042-9

Copyright © 2010 by Tim Storey
499 N. Canon Dr., Suite 400
Beverly Hills, California 90210

Published by Harrison House Publishers
P. O. Box 35035
Tulsa, Oklahoma 74153

TABLE OF CONTENTS

INTRODUCTION

Unfortunately, most people don't know that even in their darkest hours and worst failures, God is there, rooting for them and wanting to help them. Because they either forget this or never knew this, in the midst of a setback they feel like a failure and take another step back. Then another setback comes, and they take another step back. Before long they find themselves so far from where they want to be, they just give up. They can't see the light at the end of the tunnel, and they are overcome by the darkness.

Life is doing something with them instead of them doing something with life.

If you are saying to yourself, "I've stepped back so far I don't even remember where I started," just remember: It's not how you start something that counts, it's how you finish it. Even while you are feeling the sting of your setback, your comeback has already been prepared for you. You just have to begin to think about yourself and your situation in a different light.

You may be weary and don't know if you have the energy to begin again, but this may be the humble launching pad your life has been waiting for. It's too soon to give up because God hasn't given up on you. In fact, He never gives up on you. I haven't given up on you. You are the only one who can give up and abort your destiny!

There is always time for one more comeback.

How do I know this with absolute certainty? I have lived it and am continuing to live it. I have shared it with others who are living it successfully. In these chapters are the powerful truths and life-changing principles that have brought me through pain and desperation in my own life. They are what sustain me and help me to continue to move forward today.

Don't put this book down until you make a commitment to set aside a specific time and place to finish reading it. Whether it is five minutes a day or an hour a day—just do it! Read it again and again until you plant these ideas in the depths of your heart. Your comeback—and much more beyond it—are waiting for you!

1

THE INNER CRY
FOR MORE

Maybe you are in the pit of despair.

I want you to consider something. Maybe you have never thought of this, or maybe you think about this all the time. The reason you might be in despair is because you may be dissatisfied with your life. You might be surprised to know that God created you to be dissatisfied when things are not going well—and sometimes when things are going very well.

When you get off the yellow brick road and get lost or become entangled with those creepy, talking trees, it's the normal, human thing to despair and become frustrated. You know you are not where you are supposed to be, doing what you are supposed to be doing—or being who you really are.

This despair and frustration can also well up in you when everything is going fine. That is because you were created to grow and move and change yourself and everything around you for the better.

If you are like me, there are times you have no idea who you really are and what you are supposed to be doing. That is the inner cry for more! It is something God put in us so that we would reach beyond ourselves, look to Him for answers, and become better and greater. He made us, so He understands our purpose and knows all the inner workings of our hearts. He knows our every thought. Nothing gets past Him. He is the original and only Know-It-All!

He can hear you say, "Is there more to life than what I'm living?" and is pleased that you are experiencing *divine* dissatisfaction. You are shaking yourself out of complacency, out of your comfort zone, and out of any failure mentality. Don't ignore what you are feeling! That inner cry for more is simply "who you really are" making a demand on "who you have become." It is God calling you to grow up into who He created you to be and what He created you to accomplish in your life.

MOMENTUM

Momentum *expresses* your inner cry for more. It moves you forward to succeed and to be happy in life. The online Merriam-Webster dictionary says that *momentum* means "strength or force gained by motion or through the development of events."[1] We are talking about a rhythm, a pace, a stride that gains strength and force as we move forward and things happen in our lives.

Do you ever notice how much energy little kids have? Seriously, it is like they have had an IV of sugar injected into them in the middle of the night, so by the time they wake up they are raring to go! They are full of life and excited about what the new day will bring. They chase the ice cream truck, fly kites, climb trees, and splash in mud puddles. Their life is about momentum.

Kids know how to have a good time. Most of the time they are happy and run around without a care in the world. They don't stress because they know their needs will be met. On the other hand, adults can be all over the place. One minute we are up and going, and the next minute we are down and out; one minute we are happy about life, and the next minute we are discouraged. We get down and out and discouraged when setbacks cause a break in our stride, our pace, our momentum.

My goal is to help you get your momentum back if you've lost it and sustain it if you already are experiencing it. Your life isn't meant to be a series of disappointments, nor is it intended to be ordinary and stuck in a rut. However, stuff happens! You are not perfect, and thank God, He knows that. He has an extraordinary plan to bring you through the rough spots so you can keep your momentum.

GETTING YOUR BOUNCE BACK

Since your inner cry for more is expressed in momentum, what happens when you experience a setback? Momentum ceases or slows down. Sometimes it feels like the wind has been knocked out of you, and you slump over. So what can you do? You bounce back!

I read about this in Psalm 92:12 in the Bible. It says that when you trust God's plan for your life, you will not lose momentum completely. When the setback occurs and divine dissatisfaction rises up in you, you can continue to flourish like a palm tree and bear fruit even when you are old. The word "flourish" paints a picture of being in your prime, thriving, and having a bounce in your step.

A good ball has a lot of bounce. When I was growing up I used to play a lot of basketball, and one of the worst feelings was having a ball that was a little flat. It was harder to dribble, it was like passing dead weight, and it was horrible to shoot. A good ball with bounce makes the game of basketball easier and a lot more fun. The same is true in your life. When you have a lot of bounce and are flourishing, things go more smoothly and are a lot more fun. When you feel a little flat due to a setback, taking the next step feels like trying to shoot a dead basketball.

God compares us to palm trees because they bounce back. Palm trees are known for being strong and flexible. They are generally located on seacoasts, and they were designed to endure hurricanes. When 150-mile-an-hour winds blow, a palm bends. When the storm is over, it just bounces back up. God wrote that you are like a palm tree when He is your refuge. Trials or tribulations may bend you over for a while, but you always bounce back. Financial struggles may have come knocking on your door, but you bounce back. A life threatening illness may have hit your family, but you bounce back. A marriage on the verge of dissolving may be your reality, but you bounce back. Inside of you is a cry to bounce back every time the winds blow you down or you trip and fall. In His goodness and kindness, God designed you that way!

LARGE AND IN CHARGE

God created you to be large on the inside, and you are supposed to be in charge of the circumstances you encounter. In the very beginning, when He created the first man and woman, God gave them a mandate in Genesis 1:26,28: Human beings are to be productive, creative, and have *dominion* or *rule* over the Earth. That's why we have an inner cry for more inside of us. But how do we fulfill that inner cry? How do we become consistently productive and begin to rule over our circumstances?

When you buy a car, the dealer gives you an instruction manual; otherwise, you would not know all the features, capabilities, and limitations of the car. As our "manufacturer," and because He is good and kind, God has given us an instruction book for living on this planet. The Bible is His Word to us on how to live. He wrote it so we could know who He is, who we are, and what His plan for our lives and the world is. His Word is where we find the 4 P's: promises, principles, problems, and prosperity.

First of all, the Word gives us promises, and most are conditional. In general terms, if we give our lives to God, He is going to take good care of us. He promises us an abundant life of blessing and fulfillment, but we have to live by the Book! If we do things His way and honor Him in all we do, we will prosper in every area of our lives.

It's not enough to know the promises, however; we need to learn and apply His principles, overcome our problems, and thereby bring forth the prosperity He promises. We get from the promise to prosperity when we fight through the problems by using the principles in God's Word.

Psalm 1:1-3 elaborates on this very idea. God says He will bless a person who seeks the advice of those who know Him and serve Him. He will bless those who don't hang around with immoral people, and who don't sit and talk with critical, sarcastic gossips. Instead, their best friends are those who love Him and follow Him with pure hearts.

God is also going to bless those who read, study, and think about His Word day and night. As they live their lives according to His Word, these people are going to be like trees planted next to a river. They will always bear fruit in season and stay healthy year round. Everything they do will prosper. They will work *with* Him to have the abundant life Jesus died to give them. Do you see that all of this is driven by the simple inner cry for more He put in us?

DAVID HEEDED THE CRY

You have probably heard the story of David and Goliath, where the shepherd boy David slung a stone, hit the giant Goliath right between the eyes, and brought him down. However, you might not have heard the story of one of David's worst setbacks, which can be found in the book of 1 Samuel, chapter 30. Coming from war with the Philistines, David and his men returned to their families at Ziklag. When they arrived, they were told that the Amalekites had attacked the city, burned it, and taken their wives and children.

As you can imagine, David and his men were devastated. The Bible actually says they cried until they were physically exhausted. For David, it got worse. Not only was his family gone, but everyone blamed him. The men traveling with him were so angry at him for their loss, they started talking about stoning him. Talk about a bad day!

No doubt David's heart was crying out for more—more favor, more wisdom, and more courage. He was greatly distressed, he was tormented in his mind, and he felt like life was crushing him. Through all this, however, he knew he had two alternatives: He could run to *a* refuge, or he could run to *the* Refuge. He could go out and get drunk, or he could go to God. David chose to run to God. He chose to strengthen himself in the Lord. He asked Him what to do, and God gave him the answer. He told David to attack the Amalekites and everything he had lost would be recovered.

As David and his men searched for the Amalekites, they came across an Egyptian who was dehydrated and starving. After they got some food and drink into his system, he proceeded to tell them he had been a servant to someone in the Amalekite army. He had gotten sick a few days before, so his master had left him to die. He knew all about the attack at Ziklag and led David and his men right to the Amalekite camp.

David heeded the inner cry for more and made the right decision: He turned to God instead of counterfeit and temporary sources of comfort and security. Everything he had ever experienced told him that the only way to come back from a setback, to bounce back and maintain momentum, was to trust God and follow His instructions.

David did what God told him to do, and he and his men recovered all their wives and children and even got the Amalekites' flocks and herds as well. Now that's a comeback!

FIRST RESPONSE TO A SETBACK

In the beginning of this book, I encouraged you to act upon your inner cry for more, to reach up from your darkness and take the hand of God. When you take His hand, everything changes because you are embracing all His promises and principles. The Bible refers to Jesus as the Living Word, and when you give your life to Him you essentially are saying, "From now on I'm living my life by the Word. I believe You know the way. I believe You are the truth. And now You are my life."

The personal relationship you have with Jesus is the first "more" your heart is crying out for, because that relationship will give you everything else you need or want—beyond your wildest dreams. The next "more" you get is a hunger for the truth found in the Bible. You even like God's commandments! The problems in your life will continue to challenge your momentum, but now you have a firm foundation to stand on, a foundation based on His wisdom and strength instead of your own.

THE INNER CRY FOR MORE

The more you grow in your knowledge of God and His principles, the more you will be like the palm tree and bounce back. You will be like that tree planted by the river, pressing through adversity to be productive and creative and overcoming every circumstance and problem you encounter.

You are going to go from being a nervous wreck to a confident, loving, stable force to be reckoned with simply by heeding that inner cry for more and taking Jesus' hand. This is your first response to a setback!

Look up and hold on to the hand that will surely pull you out of your pit of despair and restore your momentum. Trust Him. Believe His promises. Face the fact that you are going to encounter problems. Learn His principles so you can overcome those problems. Then, one step at a time, you will move out of the pit and into the light.

2

There's Gonna Be a Fight

"I'm tired of getting beat up by life. Will it ever end?"

I hear you! There are times in our lives when we feel like problems are piled on top of problems—and they are all on our backs. That's why we need to recognize that these times are setbacks and not the end of our lives. If we recognize these times for what they are—temporary—then we can engage in the fight to move through them instead of just laying down to die.

Like a wide receiver has to fight through a whole team of defenders to catch that football and run for the touchdown, you will have to fight for your comeback. The good news is that you are not alone. God is not just cheering you on in the stands; He's out there with you!

There is something about God you need to know that will give you a lot more understanding of how He's got your back. He consists of three Persons acting as one. We can hardly wrap our minds around this, but it is the truth. The Bible calls Them the Godhead and is very clear that They are always in 100 percent agreement; They just have different functions in our lives. Each of Them is fully involved with us and our comeback.

The Father has already planned your comeback and has all the angels standing at attention to give you supernatural assistance. Jesus has already defeated your enemies and paid for every sin and mistake you have ever made by dying and then being raised from the dead. And the Holy Spirit is there to give you instructions and strength. I am also certain that He will send some people to encourage you and help you because I am one of them!

You will have to fight for your comeback, but you have the three Members of the Godhead leading you, supporting you, and supernaturally enabling you in that fight. They also are aware of something you may not have thought about: You don't want to put up a fight just to go back to the exact place and condition you were in when you fell into that pit of despair. If you do that, you will repeat the whole catastrophe! No, you want to wage a good fight, a fight to come back to a better place in a wiser and stronger condition.

God's comeback for you means you take stock of your life and clean house. You are really going to need His help for that part! Getting past your faults and weaknesses is the biggest fight you will take on, but the victories are sweeter than anything you can imagine. Fighting for your comeback is fighting to be who you were created to be, and becoming "yourself" is an amazing adventure. To do this, you need to ask the Holy Spirit to show you what caused you to fall into that pit in the first place. You may have an idea, but only He knows all of it.

There Are Reasons for Setbacks

Setbacks happen to everyone—the most successful to the least successful, the rich and the poor, the famous to the relatively unknown—and they usually happen for three reasons. If you understand how setbacks occur, you can avoid them! If a setback takes you by surprise, you can bounce back quicker by recognizing the cause and dealing with it in the right way.

1. Unexpected Circumstances. You live in a fallen, imperfect world. People around you can make bad decisions that affect you adversely. Your boss decides to lay off ten employees and you are one of them, or your teenager chooses to try drugs and gets hooked. You never would have picked these things from the menu of life if you had had a choice! You were doing a good job for your boss and taking an interest in your teenager, but both made decisions that caused you a setback.

Unexpected circumstances can also come from Mother Nature. No matter where you live in the world, bad weather or natural disasters can happen: tornadoes, hurricanes, earthquakes, tidal waves, hail, floods, drought, and forest fires, to name a few. These can cause a setback and send you right into the pit of despair.

Whether a drunk driver sideswipes your new car or a tornado blows your house down, understanding that "stuff happens" is vital to moving past your setback and coming back. This is where your faith and trust in God will see you through. If you will turn your setback over to Him, He will give you peace inside, which will enable you to hear His instructions. Remember, nothing takes Him by surprise—He's the Know-It-All! He had a comeback plan for you before the setback ever hit you.

2. Spiritual Opposition. The Bible says that God the Father is a spirit, and he has a spiritual adversary called Satan or the devil. Satan is at war with God and everyone who aligns with God—which means you. The devil also has an army of evil spirits called demons, who hate you because you are on God's side. They are all continually constructing evil schemes to trip you up. They actually have drawn up a destructive blueprint for your life based on all your faults and weaknesses.

The good news is that Jesus took care of the enemy for you! He defeated Satan through His death and resurrection, He put the Holy Spirit in you, He told the angels to bring to pass the Word and will of God that you speak, and in Luke 10:19 He said, "I have given you authority to trample on snakes and scorpions and to overcome all the power of the enemy; nothing will harm you." Now that is a great promise!

Nevertheless, you must continually be on guard, and there are times when you must take a stand or wrestle spiritual opposition to the ground until they flee. Ephesians 6:11-12 says, "Take your stand against the devil's schemes. For our struggle is not against flesh and blood, but against the rulers, against the authorities, against the powers of this dark world and against the spiritual forces of evil in the heavenly realms."

You are going to have to contend with your spiritual enemy to achieve the comeback God has ordained for you. Contending with evil spirits is like waking up in the middle of the night with too many blankets, and you feel suffocated and pressed. You need to kick that heaviness off and say, "No! In Jesus' name get off, devil!" Be aggressive with your spiritual opposition!

Let me put it to you this way: Satan and demons are terrorists. You cannot reason with them. You cannot be polite. You cannot believe a word they say, and you cannot trust them. Jesus said you are to use His name to vanquish your enemy. When you tell a demon, "In Jesus' name I command you to shut up and get out of my house!" powerful angels are immediately on the scene. Believe me, those demons are going to get out of there!

Before you get rid of your spiritual opposition, you may feel drained, fuzzy headed, or sick. After you get rid of the enemy, you are going to know the difference! Your head will clear, momentum will be restored, and peace and hope will flood even your physical body. So refuse to be intimidated by the enemy! You must stand up to him and throw him out to seize the comeback God has for you.

3. Your Bad Decisions. One of the most important principles God reveals in the Bible is that you reap what you sow. In a setback, you sowed the wind and now you are reaping the whirlwind. The seed of your first wrong action is always smaller than the harvest of its negative consequences! It is hard when *your choice* created your challenge and pain. Thank God for His mercy and grace!

Recognizing and dealing with your bad decisions, taking responsibility for your self-centered, selfish words and actions— that is what separates the men and women from the boys and girls. This is probably the hardest to face of the three reasons for setbacks. It's a lot easier to blame your problems on another person, the weather, or the devil! It takes character and courage to allow God to show you the brutal, honest truth about yourself.

Some people are so focused on what they want, they don't even know they have had a setback. A friend of mine who is an NFL linebacker, was hit hard in a playoff game and broke his thumb. He was so caught up in the intensity of the game, he didn't know it was broken until eight plays later. By that time, one of the other players noticed his thumb was dangling from his hand, bleeding.

My friend's adrenaline was so high he hadn't felt the pain. That is the way you may be. You don't know you have been injured because you have been numbed by the trauma, or else you are living life in the fast lane and haven't slowed down long enough to let yourself feel the pain. My friend had to realize that his thumb was broken before he could get the help he needed and be restored.

You must recognize the setback before you can have a comeback.

I'll let you in on the secret to coming back from bad decisions that have caused you and possibly those around you grief: the blood of Jesus. You read it right! Jesus shed His *innocent* blood for your *guilty* blood. He was sinless and you are not, so He paid the debt for your sin—even your most horrible thoughts and actions. Because of Jesus' shed blood, God forgives you; and only His forgiveness will set you free from all the shame, guilt, and condemnation associated with what you did wrong.

Do you see that when Jesus died for you, He knew you would do what you have done? He knew *then* what you would do *now*. He died knowing this. He loves you regardless of your performance, and this is the key to gratefully and humbly receiving the comeback God has already prepared for you.

Sometimes the biggest fight is with yourself. You have to fight to receive God's forgiveness, forgive yourself, and to forgive anyone else involved. Let me tell you from experience: It is well worth the fight!

DEFINING A COMEBACK

So what is a comeback? My definition is that it is a return to a place of stature, significance, and well-being with the Lord. I'm not talking about a manmade comeback plan; I'm talking about God's comeback plan. You will never truly come back without His forgiveness and peace. *A real comeback is inward as well as outward.*

You may be asking yourself, "Well what's wrong with my plan? Why do I have to get all introspective? Can't I just do the right thing and go on?" Unfortunately your vision is too clouded to do the right thing or devise a great comeback plan. You can only see what your setback allows you to see. A man at the bottom of a deep well cannot see anything but darkness and the sky far above him. He cannot see the surrounding landscape. He doesn't know what awaits him once he climbs out of that well.

Most people attempt what I call, "The Clouded Comeback." It's called a clouded comeback because no matter how sincere their efforts on the outside, their inside is troubled by shame, grief, guilt, fear, lies, anger, confusion, anxiety, and other negative thoughts and emotions. Setbacks can overwhelm people on the inside, so they try to escape those volatile and frightening thoughts and feelings by doing, doing, doing on the outside.

Initially, escapism creates a comeback you think you can handle and control, but in the end it will fail because what is going on inside hasn't changed. Please understand that mere goal setting, great motivation, and determination will not be enough! The real fight for your comeback is on the inside. That's why I say that a core comeback is needed. A core comeback originates on the inside and transforms the outside.

YOUR CORE COMEBACK

The core is the center of something. Your core is your heart and spirit. It is who you really are; and no matter how hard you try to be different, who you really are is eventually going to come out! The Bible puts it this way, "As he thinks in his heart, so is he" (Proverbs 23:7 NKJV). That is why you need a *core* comeback. You need to deal with the root issues that caused your setback, or you will just go out and do the same things again.

There is only One Person who can get to the root issues in your heart that have caused your setback—and maybe one setback after another. That person is Jesus. He is the Refuge who loves you, accepts you, and understands you completely. He knows what is going on in the core of your being. You only have an idea, if that. You can choose to change, but real change only happens when you turn over your entire being to Jesus. Then He can change you on the inside so you can stop repeating the same mistakes on the outside.

A Core Comeback is God-inspired.

Did you know that when you breathe air, you are inspiring? Inspiration is breathing in the atmosphere around you, and whatever you breathe in will determine the health and productivity of your physical body. In the same way, what you breathe in spiritually, intellectually, and emotionally will determine what you think, feel, say, and do. When you are inspired you are taking in ideas and emotions that will either move you forward or push you back. You don't want to inhale smoke and toxic fumes physically, and you don't want to inhale lies and perversion mentally, emotionally, and spiritually.

When God inspires you, He literally breathes into you His love, truth, and power. His love reminds you how valuable and important you are. His truth dispels the lies and deception of the enemy that have held you captive all these years. His power gives you the strength and confidence to step out in faith and be who He created you to be.

This reminds me of the balloon man at the county fair. He takes a seemingly shapeless balloon, blows into it, and shapes it into an animal. In the same way, when God breathes into your life, your heart and mind begin to take the shape your were meant to take. If you are the balloon, you cannot blow into yourself! That is how fruitless and pointless it is to try to inspire yourself. God created you to be inspired and filled by Him. He wants to breathe His love, truth, and power into you, to inspire you to rise in life and reach your full potential.

A Core Comeback is God-endorsed.

God wants your comeback more than you do. He has placed all His resources behind it, He has planned it before you needed it, and He sent Jesus to die for you so He could give you everything you need for it. He has not only endorsed your comeback, but also He is counting on it! You are His child and a part of His divine plan. All you have to do is give Him your life, and He will personally see to it that you are fulfilled and successful.

If you could put on special goggles to see into the spiritual realm, you would see how God has endorsed your comeback. You would see the army of angels that is just waiting for your prayers and declarations of faith. When you endorse what God has endorsed, it will be done!

It's very important that you become convinced of God's desire and ability to give you a core comeback. To be convinced is to have faith, and God tells us that He is looking for people with faith in Him and His promises. It's really very simple. When you have faith in Him, you give Him permission to change you on the inside, to move you on the outside, and to clear the way for you to move forward. That is your core comeback.

I'll tell you what you will have to fight against: Doing it on your own. Doing what your friends inspire you to do. Doing what your culture endorses. Doing your life according to everyone and everything but God. You are going to have to fight to stick with His plan instead of someone else's—including your own!

DON'T GET STUCK IN THE SETBACK!

Let me tell you what will happen if you choose not to fight for your comeback: you will get stuck in your setback. Then, if you sit long enough in your setback, you will become cemented in it. That means you will become rigid, unbending, and unwilling to change or grow. You will become frozen in time, a relic of an unfortunate past, with no relevance to others today or in the future.

Have you ever spoken to someone who has become cemented in a setback? You will see it in their posture, on their countenance, in their words, and in their energy level. It's like something has sucked the life out of them.

If you have ever been in a setback, you know how hard it is to break free from it. You see that big old Bible sitting by your bed, and you know that it contains what you need. Yet, you are so overwhelmed and depleted of hope and strength that you just sit there, looking at it. Finally, you roll over and fall asleep, only to wake up the next day feeling worse.

Do you know how many times I wanted to quit, to just sit back in my setback and wallow in self-pity? I was tired of all the cheap shots and battles with the enemy, other people—and myself. One day I was walking through Dallas-Fort Worth Airport so tired my feet were dragging ten steps behind me. The comeback coach needed a comeback! My hair was a mess and I hadn't shaved, so I had my hat pulled down as far as it would go and I had my sunglasses on. My head was down so I wouldn't have to see or talk to anybody. I was in one of those "don't mess with me" moods.

It takes a lot to get me that way because I am up 90 percent of the time, but I was not feeling good that day—and that's usually the time when God pulls a sneaky trick on me! A little lady came running up to me calling, "Tim Storey!"

I thought, *Oh no! Not today.* I said, "Yeah?" looking through my sunglasses and wishing they made me invisible.

She blurted out, "I was dying of cancer and you encouraged me that I didn't have to give up...and guess what? I didn't. That was several years ago and I'm still alive!"

At that moment I knew I could run, I could hide, but God would find me. He would find me and inspire me. He would endorse my comeback. He would send a stranger if he had to, but he would give me hope—the hope that I was still valued and loved. My gifts and talents were not just to make me look good; they were to help others live life to the fullest.

Even then, I could have chosen to reject God's outstretched hand. It's a scary thought, but I could have chosen to remain cemented in my setback. I'm so grateful I didn't! I'm so glad I chose to come out from behind the wall of my sunglasses and receive the hope He was offering me through that woman.

TURN YOUR MESS INTO A MESSAGE

You cannot stay cemented in your setback either. Somebody needs you! I don't care how far you think you have sunk into the pit of despair, how desperately you have failed, how tragic your circumstances are, or how badly you are hurting; somebody needs your testimony, your wisdom, your strength, your talents, and your encouragement.

Part of God's comeback for you includes fighting for someone else to come back.

Did you know that one of God's objectives in fighting for your comeback and getting you out of your setback is to help someone else? People have caught on to this principle, whether they know Him or not. That's why there are so many support groups— Mothers Against Drunk Drivers, Alcoholics Anonymous, and Alzheimer's Caregivers, to name a few. When you refuse to get stuck in your setback and allow God to inspire and endorse your comeback, your mess becomes a message of hope to those who need it. Your comeback becomes part of their comeback.

While in the inner city of Los Angeles, a young man who was obviously in the drug world came up for prayer. I watched him and could see destiny inside him. I looked into his bloodshot eyes and said, "Why are you here?"

Out of his heart he cried, "I don't want to be a loser! I don't want to be a loser! You said I can be a winner! All my life I've been a loser!"

The real person inside him was begging to be released. His destiny and God-given purpose had been bottled up long enough and were crying to come out. The moment he made Jesus his Refuge, his life began to change radically. He got free from the drugs and started following us around to other meetings. We continued to teach him and helped him get out of his setback. His comeback involved helping other inner city kids who needed the mess of his past life to be a message of hope for them. His comeback inspired them to fight for their comeback.

Another great example that you may know about is Duane Chapman, known as the reality TV star Dog the Bounty Hunter. He is no stranger to hardships, adversities, and setbacks. This highly intense, fugitive hunting, bail bondsman has never lacked for "bouncing back."

By the time Dog was twenty-four, he had already used his charismatic personality to cause chaos, racking up nineteen criminal convictions. Eighteen were for armed robbery, and he was beginning to serve a five-year prison term for first-degree murder. He spent the first year and a half feeling the despair of a setback within the cold walls of a Texas prison.

Just as Dog was feeling the lowest of the low, God moved on his heart to change his ways. He made a vow that when he was released from prison, he would make America a safer place. Instead of hunting for trouble, he would hunt for those who made trouble and bring them in to the authorities.

God turned Dog from a zero to a hero. Although he still felt the sting of shame from the public and his family, he proceeded to take over six thousand fugitives off the streets and then landed a television show about his exploits in 2004. Dog beat the odds. Instead of getting lost in a lifestyle of setbacks, he chose to fight for his comeback, making it his passion to find others who were also in need of a comeback.

If you have seen his TV show, you know it is quite amusing and inspiring. After he has made a capture, he reads the criminal his rights and then gives them a motivational speech! He encourages them to change their lifestyle and make better choices. Dog is now a comeback coach!

I must be honest with you. It isn't easy to come back. It will take some sweat and some tears. Sometimes you will feel like you are in a war, but you are never alone, and help and hope are available to you. There is no mistake too large, pain too unbearable, or story too unremarkable that God cannot turn it into a comeback story. So don't give up in the depths of despair. Lift your head high, even when you haven't a clue as to what you are supposed to do. Look up and ask Jesus to begin your core comeback, and then fight for it! Fight for your comeback, and you will be an inspiration to others who need a comeback too.

3

TURN, TURN, TURN

"I guess you're saying I have to make some major changes inside, like how I think and what I believe about myself, about God, and about why I'm alive. I just don't know if I can do that. I've made so many bad choices!"

Today is the first day of the rest of your life. You are a mighty person in the making, a masterpiece in progress, a miracle in motion. Although you may have made many mistakes in your past, God still has a great plan for your future—if you will do things His way. If you let Him, He will mold you into a vessel of honor for His purposes. He will breathe life into you and change you.

Years ago a rock band called The Byrds recorded a song called "Turn, Turn, Turn," which became a big hit. The word "turn" indicates a change of direction. The chorus said, "To every thing turn, turn, turn. There is a season; turn, turn, turn." The folk singer Pete Seeger wrote the song, but he took most of the lyrics from the Bible, from Ecclesiastes 3:1-8 KJV:

To every thing there is a season,

and a time to every purpose under the heaven:

A time to be born, and a time to die;

a time to plant, and a time to pluck up that which is planted;

A time to kill, and a time to heal;

a time to break down, and a time to build up;

A time to weep, and a time to laugh;

a time to mourn, and a time to dance;

A time to cast away stones, and a time to gather stones together;

a time to embrace, and a time to refrain from embracing;

A time to get, and a time to lose;

a time to keep, and a time to cast away;

A time to rend, and a time to sew;

a time to keep silence, and a time to speak;

A time to love, and a time to hate;

a time of war, and a time of peace.

Sometimes it is hard to turn from one season to the next, especially if the season you are entering is not a pleasant one. When you have a setback, you have to *turn* to a season of self-examination, reflection, and changing direction. Then, after you have allowed God to show you the root issues that caused your setback, after you have taken care of old business that needed to be dealt with for you to move ahead, you must *turn to enter* the new season.

A biblical principle you must live by in order to get your comeback is this: No matter what you have lived through, what wrong decisions you have made, or what challenges are staring you in the face, make a decision not to poison your future with the pain of the past. Don't spend time dwelling on old events, situations, and conversations that you and God have already settled. It would be a shame if God showed you the next step in front of you, but you couldn't see it because you were looking behind you.

There is a story in the Old Testament of a guy who had to *turn* to get past his past and do what was right for a change. If you think you are too messed up to be useful in any way, I think his story will change your mind!

AN UNLIKELY HERO

There was a Jewish man in the Bible named Gideon who had to *turn* from the past and embrace the new season. You can read his story in the book of Judges, chapters 6 through 8. He began as a simple, somewhat cowardly man who was just trying to get by in life. At that time, the nation of Israel was being bullied by the nation of Midian and Gideon was hiding, trying to avoid any confrontation with the Midianites.

One day an angel tapped Gideon on the shoulder and said, "You're the man who's going to whip the Midianites and run them off your turf. So get ready! And don't worry about a thing. This was God's idea. He's with you all the way."

Gideon's response was, "No way! And if God's so great, how come He let those Midianites invade our land in the first place?

Where's He been while we've been going through all this stuff? I heard about the great things He did for us years ago, like when He parted the Red Sea and drowned our enemies behind us, so where is He when we need a miracle today, huh?"

It's just so easy to point the finger at God when the bottom drops from underneath us or we face challenges that are hard to swallow. Maybe it's a life-threatening illness or not enough money to pay the bills. Perhaps our marriage is on the rocks or our child is unmanageable. The real big one is a natural disaster. It must be God if our house gets struck by lightning or our car floats away in a flood! It couldn't just be the Earth doing its thing.

After we blame God, then we ask, "Why? Why did You do this to me?" If we are really holy and reverent, we will ask a little more politely, "Why did You *allow* this to happen?" Like Gideon, we are not really interested in the truth; we are just feeling sorry for ourselves, playing the blame game, and making the most of our setback.

Gideon needed to *turn* from nursing, cursing, and rehearsing his problems and release his setback to God. Then God could reveal his comeback. In Gideon's case, God was merciful and gave Gideon an assignment. I think He did this because He knew it would give him the momentum to achieve his comeback.

Gideon did what so many of us do when we get an assignment: he started listing all of his limitations and the reasons why he couldn't do it. He said, "I mess up everything I do. My family's a wreck. I'm a nobody—totally uneducated. I'm a coward. Why do You think I'm hiding in this stinking wine cellar? Man, I can't even show my face on the street!"

The angel ignored Gideon's whining and complaining and said, "Get over it. This is your big break. You can be 'the man' and save the day for your family, your friends, and the whole nation. Think how that's going to look on your resume. I'm telling you, the Big Guy is sending you, and He's given you everything you need to do it."

No Fear!

Our limitations scare *us*, but they don't intimidate *God*. He knows our flaws, and He's big enough to fill our weaknesses with His strength and cover our mistakes with His mercy. Because He wants to be our partner and supernaturally empower us, He always gives us a dream that's way too big for us. He is a God of faith! You cannot please Him without having faith. So when we dream beyond our own ability and buy into His plan, we *turn* from fear and step out in faith. At that point we know He's going to have to come through for it to happen—and that is just what He is waiting for!

In his wildest dreams, Gideon could not imagine how he was going to drive out those mean Midianites who had been terrorizing the neighborhood for years. He didn't see himself as a "mighty man of valor," but God did; and you may not be able to see yourself as a masterpiece, but God does.

In order for you to *turn* and step out in faith like Gideon did, you have to understand how much God loves you. He doesn't point His finger at you or hold onto His anger because you blew it. He knows all about your past, but He forgives you because Jesus paid the price for your sins. Once you *turn* from your sin and get right with Him about it, He forgives you and then forgets what you did!

God doesn't treat you as your actions deserve. He doesn't even remember them, so you don't have to drag all that junk from the past around with you anymore. Accepting His forgiveness enables you to move forward with peace, and forgiving yourself enables you to move forward with confidence. Your faith in Him and knowing His love for you is the key to having no fear.

Once Gideon *turned* from his fears and stepped out in faith to defeat the Midianites, he was on his way to not only his comeback but also the comeback of the whole nation of Israel! He went from setback to comeback and beyond. If you read this story in the Bible, you will have the same thought I did: *If God can work with a dysfunctional coward like Gideon, He can do something with me! If Gideon could make that turn from his past, then I can too.*

GOD KNOWS YOUR FRAME

God will help you *turn* from the past because He knows you better than anyone else. The Bible says He knows your *frame*, which is your physical structure, your mental and emotional makeup, your personality—the good, the bad, and the ugly! Your frame is the way you are put together, and you are unique. For example, if you were born and raised in Sweden, you are going to be different from someone born and raised in California in the USA. If you went to engineering school, your perspective is going to be different from someone who went to a music conservatory. Yet, when people come to Jesus, we think they should all be exactly alike.

Obviously, there should be some similarities among Christians. We should all reflect the character and power of Jesus. But we even reflect Jesus in different ways, and it takes time for us to begin to do that. We need to cut each other some slack as we grow up in God. That's what God did for Gideon, and we need to learn to accept and love our brothers and sisters—and ourselves—like He does.

Although we all should be marching to the beat of the same Drummer, Christians don't always look alike, talk alike, or act alike. We are coming from different perspectives and backgrounds, but that is where it gets interesting. We have similar setbacks, we have to fight for our comebacks, and to go beyond our own abilities we need God and each other. God made us this way!

Perhaps you weren't raised in a happy, Christian home. Who knows the hell you may have gone through? It doesn't make sense that the second you become a Christian and join a church, we expect you to be perfect. Your frame is different from everyone else—and yet it is also similar. So you can find common ground with other believers in the Spirit and the Word, but then you express truth and compassion in your own unique way. God understands this. He knows your frame because He is trying to *turn* you.

THE POTTER AND THE CLAY

God is the potter and you are the clay. He understands clay! He knows just how much water you need to be transformed into His masterpiece. He knows how to *turn* you on His potter's wheel and mold you into the person He created you to be. It may not feel so good at times, but eventually you realize that it's easier if the clay just surrenders to the hands of the potter. Some masterpieces take longer than others, but in God's hands they are all masterpieces!

If you have seen *The Ten Commandments* or read the book of Exodus, you know the story of Moses. God talked to him from a burning bush and gave him his assignment. Moses cried, "I can't go back to Egypt! I killed a man. And besides, I can't talk straight anymore."

God said, "Been there—done that! I did it with Abraham, Isaac, and Jacob. When I gave them their assignments, Abraham was worshipping the moon, Isaac had a lot of family problems, and Jacob was a deceiver. No one will ever be qualified because I created humans to need me. To turn from the faults and failures of your past, Moses, you need me—and I love that! I love it when we do things together."

No one understands you better than God, including you! Even knowing your worst faults and failures, He will never leave you nor forsake you. No matter what you did in the past, He forgives you and is waiting for you to take the next step with Him. Whatever assignment He gives you, trust Him. Some of the greatest songs were written in the darkest hours of those who were inspired by the only One who believed in them!

If you haven't already, surrender your entire being to the Master Potter. Allow Him to *turn* you on His wheel of salvation and restoration. He will release your uniqueness and give you peace and fulfillment as no one else can.

THREE KINDS OF PEOPLE

Over the years of ministering to people, I have noticed that it is harder for some to surrender to the Potter's hand and allow Him to turn their lives around. Of the different kinds of people, there is one kind that we can all become, and this kind is able to turn from their setbacks to obtain their comebacks.

There are three kinds of people: the idealist, the pessimist, and the realist. Idealists can be in the middle of a hellhole they created and think they are going to get out overnight. They are $300,000 in debt, watch a real estate infomercial, and are convinced that buying that piece of property will "reverse the curse" immediately. It isn't going to happen.

The idealist may be as round as he is tall, sitting in his recliner, watching television, eating a triple-meat, extra-large pizza. He hollers to his wife, who is in bed trying to sleep, "Baby, order that thing for me. Call the number right now, 1-800-GET-THIN!" He thinks it's going to hit him with "instant skinny" just like the commercial.

Another sure sign of an idealist is someone who always has a crazy slogan for everything. It's good to be optimistic and to think positive, but an idealist does not see reality at all. They oversimplify problems and solutions. They pervert faith into fantasy. Faith apart from works is fantasy. You will never turn from your setback like this!

Then there's the pessimist. They always see the negative side of things, like one of those little guys in Jonathan Swift's *Gulliver's Travels*. Gulliver is a great big guy, but no matter what happens this tiny guy always says, "We'll never make it!" Even when the odds are good and the future looks bright, a pessimist will find the cloud in the silver lining.

Another identifying statement of a pessimist is, "Yes, but...." You're headed to the beach and the sun is shining bright without a cloud in the sky. The pessimist will sit in the backseat saying, "Yes, but it still could rain." A pessimist has a negative state of mind, which is the opposite of God's state of mind. He is the God of all possibilities!

Pessimism cancels faith. Since God is looking for faith, pessimism will turn God and His miracles away. This is not the turn you are after! The only way you are going to go from your setback to your comeback and beyond is with the supernatural help of God. Every comeback orchestrated by God is miraculous, so you have to have faith. You cannot be a pessimist and come back.

Lastly, we come to the realist. Realists see the obvious but are willing to devise a plan to correct the problem. They recognize when a turn is called for. They say, "Yes, I made a mistake when I made that investment. I never really had peace in my heart about it, and I should have done more research to see what God was trying to tell me. Next time I'll do it His way!" And they turn!

The realist understands the bottom line: God is real, and only He can make your comeback real. To get past your past, you must face the reality of your situation and then look to God for the next step. Remember, He has already prepared your comeback. You just need to *turn* and take that first step of faith, and then the next step of faith. He will do the rest, and it will be miraculous!

Get Real

You may have some huge, obvious problems in your life. It may be the car you drive or the body you're in. It could be your financial situation or your marriage. Turning from your past doesn't mean shoving all your problems in a closet and never dealing with them. Turning from your past requires you to clean your closet! Otherwise, every day you will walk by that closet door and be haunted by what's behind it.

A setback indicates that it's time to get real. An angel is probably not going to wash your car while you are at work, and most likely, God is not going to strike you with a lightning bolt that takes off fifty pounds and leaves you in perfect health. No, that car is going to stay dirty unless you wash it or pay someone else to wash it, and your health and fitness are directly proportional to what you do about them.

This involves a principle I call the Law of the Harvest. It comes from Proverbs 12:11, which basically says that people who work toward their goals and dreams will have abundance, but people who just dream and don't do anything are acting crazy. They are crazy because they expect a harvest when they haven't planted one seed.

Farmers get this. It is stupid to expect a great harvest by just looking at a field. You pray for good weather, and you step out in faith. You plow, you plant, you fertilize, and you water if the rains don't come. The assignment to produce food is God's assignment. So farmers do their part and have faith God will do His part.

God likes to work *through us* and *with us* not just *for us*. Life is a partnership. Plowing is laborious so you need His strength. Pursuing your comeback is hard work at times. Planting is depositing, and you can't deposit anything you don't have. You must acquire the seed. Fill yourself with the Living Word to stay encouraged and to encourage others. Watering produces growth. You will notice all the ways you have changed because you stayed disciplined.

Finally, you reap! Reaping is receiving the harvest God has prepared for you. This is when you achieve your comeback and He reveals what is just beyond it. You see, God is always *turning* you toward bigger and better things. You will never stay in one place for long when you partner with Him. There are many seasons to experience!

Following the Law of the Harvest is a sure sign that you aren't a pessimist or an idealist; you are a realist who trusts in the

Lord. You *turn* when you need to. You get real and deal with your problems. You get God's plan and step out in faith, confident something miraculous will happen. You clean your house and get free inside. You take that step of faith in your assignment, drawing on His strength and ability, and things you only dreamed of begin to actually happen.

To get out of your setback, you will have to *turn*.

4

GROWING PAINS

"Change is so hard. I am beginning to see some difference, but it is taking everything I have to keep going."

Let me tell you the simple truth: No pain—no gain. That is the slogan for anyone who accomplished anything at any time in history. It is a fact that, because we live in an imperfect world, we encounter great resistance whenever we try to change ourselves or the world around us for the better. Often we are our own worst enemy, or our spiritual enemies trip us up. Whatever the obstacle there is usually a struggle involved, and sometimes there is pain.

I remember being a kid growing up and now I have kids who are growing up. It's not easy. Physically, there are aches and pains as the body changes shape and gets bigger. There are intellectual learning curves and emotional adjustments. This natural experience of growing pains is parallel to our spiritual experience. Growing up in God also involves some pain for gain—like going from a setback to a comeback and beyond.

There are two people in the Bible who always inspire me to keep growing and fighting for my comeback no matter how painful it is. At their lowest point in life, this husband and wife watched their newborn son's life fade away. There was nothing they could do about it. I have lost family members who were very dear to me, and honestly, helplessly watching your child die is probably the worst setback any human being can face. Yet, this couple came back.

DAVID AND BATHSHEBA

Years after he killed Goliath the giant and overcame his setback at Ziklag, David finally became the king of Israel. It was after he achieved great success that he had his biggest setback—and this is so common! It happens too often. Someone works hard, going from setback to comeback again and again, their dreams are coming true, people look to them as a role model or even a hero, and suddenly they fall to the ground in pieces like Humpty Dumpty. That's what happened to King David.

You can read the story in 2 Samuel, chapters 11 and 12. It began with one bad decision: When David was supposed to fight a war, he stayed home. That was the initial bad decision that led to all the others. Have you ever noticed that a setback usually begins with a seemingly insignificant decision? You sense what you are doing is not right, but you think it's not that big a deal. Well, David simply decided not to go to war that year.

Because he was at home with nothing to do, King David began partying all night and sleeping all day. One night he was bored on the roof of his palace, drinking wine and looking over the city, when he saw Bathsheba taking a bath on her roof. Now Bathsheba was totally innocent. She knew all the men were at war, and she had no idea the king had stayed home.

David was creating his own setbacks, but Bathsheba was about to experience a series of tragic setbacks because of someone else's bad decisions. She was shocked when the king summoned her to the palace and sexually forced himself on her. Later, she discovered she was pregnant with his child.

When Bathsheba told David she was carrying his child, he immediately tried to cover the evidence of his sin by summoning her husband Uriah home from the battlefield. He told Uriah to spend a few nights with his wife, but Uriah was so loyal to his king and the men who still were fighting for their lives, he refused to go home and enjoy his wife. Even when David got him drunk, he still slept in the king's doorway!

In an attempt to hide one sin, David committed another. He ordered his general to put Uriah on the front lines, where he was certain to be killed. After Uriah was dead and Bathsheba's mourning period was over, David married her. He thought he was free and clear until the prophet Nathan came knocking on his door.

When believers reach a certain point in their sin, God will always send a Nathan to them. This is the person who asks you to dinner and says, "Hey, I know you're in trouble. God told me. Do you want to talk about it?" If you're smart, you will recognize God's helping hand and get real! That's what David did. He listened when Nathan told him the jig was up. God was loving, but He was also just; so there were going to be consequences for David's sin. The worst was that the child Bathsheba was carrying would die.

David fell on his face before the Lord, confessing his sin and pleading for the life of his son. Can you imagine the guilt and shame he was feeling? He had raped a woman, gotten her pregnant, murdered her husband (whom she loved), forced her to marry him, and now the child she was carrying would die because of his sins.

Can you imagine the storm of emotions Bathsheba was feeling? She had no legal recourse against the man who had raped her, impregnated her, killed the husband she loved, and then forced her to marry him. Now the child she just bore was dead because of him. Hatred, fear, and grief are probably just a few of the emotions Bathsheba was battling.

The situation of David and Bathsheba was like the worst soap opera you could imagine—but it happened to real people! After their baby died, you would think David and Bathsheba would never want to go near one another again, but these two were different from most people. They turned to God for a miracle comeback. They knew if they did this, the mess they created would be a setback and not the end of their lives. As a result, over the years they developed a great marriage relationship.

David and Bathseba's marriage was a miracle comeback, but that was not the last of their setbacks or their pain. David's other children made terrible decisions and caused both of them a lot of grief through the years. They had one setback after another and one comeback after another. Going from a setback to a comeback is not a one-time deal!

You may be in the biggest mess imaginable and think nothing could be worse. Hopefully, this is the worst setback you will ever face, but I guarantee you that it probably will not be the last. I can also guarantee that God has a comeback for every setback you face. To Him, every pain is an opportunity for great gain, and He is always ready to fill your weakness with His strength. Understanding this truth will help you through the growing pains!

TURN TO GOD

Great men and women like David and Bathsheba turned to God for help. They knew it was humanly impossible for them to succeed unless God turned their weaknesses to strengths—and that means a growth process took place. Their miracle didn't happen overnight, and yours won't either. No one grows six feet in a year in the natural, and you are not going to grow into the character and power of Jesus in a year either.

Let's say one of your weaknesses is being moody, and one day you decide to turn from moodiness to the joy of the Lord. From that day, every time you begin that familiar downward spiral, you turn over all your emotions to God. Maybe you were moody every day last year, and after a month of turning it over to God, you find you are only moody every other day. That's growth! That's gain. If you're just a little better each day or each week, eventually your weakness will become a strength. So don't focus on the pain of overcoming your weakness, *focus on the gain of your increasing strength.*

I'm not talking to your mind; I'm talking to your spirit, your heart on the inside of you. This is where your weakness grows into strength. Whether your weakness is an addiction, a bad temper, or poor work habits, by God's power you are turning it over to Him and He is enabling you to turn a corner in your life. He is nudging you to keep growing one step at a time so you get better each day.

Life feels so good when you know you are changing for the better, when you see you have turned a corner. All of a sudden one day you realize you are happy, not moody. You need to own that joy! It's okay to be proud that you are taking positive steps forward. Pat yourself on the back! Your efforts are reaping a harvest!

You also need to guard that joy. There will be tons of things coming at you like bullets, so stay close to God. Guard your heart, your thoughts, and your relationships. If you were raised in chaos, chaos became your frame of reference and culture. Chaos made you moody. Now, when you find yourself experiencing some peace and joy, don't go back and play past videos. That's how you sabotage your victories. If you still have to associate with those who live in chaos, you can choose not to participate. God will give you the wisdom and courage to turn away from it.

Old relationships will try to wrap themselves around you and pull you back into your old ways of living. Don't let it happen! God wants to connect you with people who will understand your growing pains and help you, not hinder you. You are not locked into anything, and you will gain self-respect by seeing yourself through God's eyes instead of your old friends' eyes.

Lastly, as you turn to God and begin to grow, always remember to give your joy away. Other people are in need of the happiness you possess. Don't you agree that being around people who are genuinely happy is an encouragement and a breath of fresh air? It's contagious and usually infects others. Isn't it great that when you turn to God, exchanging your weakness for His strength, everyone around you gets the benefit of it?

Big Waves Happen

I was bodysurfing in Hawaii on a sandy beach. The waves were huge, and I wasn't used to the currents and undertow. A wave would hit and knock me down. Before I could get up, another wave would come and hit me again. Finally, the force of a wave pulled my swimsuit clean off me! I had to swim around and find my swimsuit before I could go to shore, all the while still being hit with those big waves. Does that describe your life right now?

You get hit, are almost standing, and bam! You get hit again. Sometimes it knocks your drawers off! Now you not only have the waves hitting you, but you've got to look for your drawers.

You feel like yelling, "Stop already! Just leave me alone! I don't want to change. I like me just the way I am." When growing pains come in big waves, you have to remind yourself of the great gain that is ahead of you. You have to remember who you are: You are a trailblazer, a world-shaker, and a history maker. With God, you will work through it!

Even while you're feeling the sting of a setback—*I can't believe I have cancer,* or *I can't believe he left me,* or *I can't believe I didn't get that job*—God is getting you ready, preparing you for your comeback. He didn't send the adversity, but He is using it to your advantage. If you are plugged into Him, He is bringing forth the real you—the "you" you have always wanted to be!

Notice I said "if" you are plugged into God? By that I mean you have to stay in contact with Him, get to know Him, talk to Him. "But I don't know how to hear His voice." It's as simple as this: stop, look, and listen. "Stop" refers to not being so busy. Maybe you need to slow your pace and set aside a certain time every day for just you and God. Good communication usually takes place during quiet times, not hectic ones.

"Look" means look to God. Don't rely on friends, family, books, or TV shows as your source of comfort. They can fail but He can't. "Listen" to what He says. Get quiet and hear His peace-filled whisper in your heart. Pick up His Word and read until the words leap off the page into your heart. For some of us who have a hard time sitting still, this might be one of the most painful parts of growing up!

Whether the big waves are crashing upon you or you have clear sailing, you need to make your relationship with God your first priority. Sometimes He will lead you to ride those waves to shore; other times He will have you swim around in the water until you find your drawers! Either way, when you are plugged in to an all-knowing, all-powerful God, you won't be overtaken.

Learning to Talk Right

Being a public speaker, I know that public humiliation can be just a couple of brash words away—and that is painful! However, whenever my mouth trips me up, I have to learn from it. It took me a while to learn to talk like my parents when I was a child, and it's taking me a while to learn to talk in the style of Jesus.

Jesus talked a lot about talking! He taught that we can change our lives and our environment by the words we speak. Have you ever walked into a room and felt peace in the air? The reason for that is that the people in that room were speaking words to cause an atmosphere of peace. Proverbs 18:21 states this principle in really blatant terms: "The tongue has the power of life and death." Read Genesis, chapter 1, and you will see that God *spoke* the world into existence. You are made in His image, so you speak your world into existence too.

Remember the old saying, "What you say is what you get"? I like to say, "You'll never reach the palace by talking like a peasant." The late Christopher Reeve and his wife Dana understood this. He truly was a "super man" and she a "super woman" in my opinion. After the terrible horseback riding accident that left him paralyzed and breathing on a respirator, Christopher questioned the value of his life. He mouthed these words to his wife Dana, "Maybe we should let me go."

She said, "I will support whatever you want to do because this is your life and your decision. But I want you to know that I'll be with you for the long haul, no matter what. You're still you, and I love you."[1]

Her words framed Christopher's decision not to step back from life in the midst of what appeared to be a devastating setback. Yes, he remained paralyzed, but he didn't sit still for a moment! He fought his way through his setback and worked with researchers around the world to look for a solution for spinal cord injuries. We saw him in the political arena, at the Academy Awards, and as a spokesman for various charities. He also published a book entitled, *Still Me*, coined from Dana's powerful words.

Here's a revelation you need to get in your spirit and your heart: When you believe what God says about your situation, you will begin to change what you say about it; and when you begin to speak what God says about it, it will happen. Believe that God can do what He said He would do. He has quite a track record after all. He made Heaven and Earth, He gave 100-year-old Abraham and 90-year-old Sarah a son, He parted the Red Sea for Moses, and He calmed the stormy sea for Jesus. I can testify that He still heals the sick and opens blind eyes. Don't you think, if He did all that, He can do what He has said He will do for you?

GROWING PAINS

If you don't know how to believe for what looks impossible, get around those who do. I'm not talking about idealists who walk in fantasy and presumption; I'm talking about those who know God, who believe His Word and walk by His Spirit. There is a big difference! First, they know what God's Word says and what His will is. They are not ruled by what they want but what He wants, and their words and actions reflect that commitment.

People with real faith in God and His promises dare to believe the impossible and have the courage to see the invisible. They will always tell you, "Follow God, and everything's going to be all right." Their faith and positive belief system will get inside of you.

If you are going to speak your world into existence—the dynamic, fantastic world God has for you—then you are going to have to fill your heart with the right beliefs and thoughts, just like you fill your car's gas tank with the right kind of fuel. Plug in to people who will wake you up, stir you up, help you up, and shake you up. Cultivate friends who have the life and power of God pouring out of them!

Growing pains are hard, especially when you are changing the way you talk about things, but they bring forth the stature and character of God in your life. More and more, you will realize the power in your words. You will understand that "what goes in will come out" and be more careful about what you hear, see, and believe.

God is big. Fill up with His principles for life and His dreams for your life. Believe them in your heart, speak them in faith, and take the first step of faith He tells you to take. I like how Jesus put it in Mark 11:22-24: "'Have faith in God,' Jesus answered. 'I tell you the truth, if anyone says to this mountain, "Go, throw yourself into the sea," and does not doubt in his heart but believes that what he says will happen, it will be done for him. Therefore I tell you, whatever you ask for in prayer, believe that you have received it, and it will be yours.'"

The first thing Jesus said was, "Have faith in God." Everything else comes out of your intimacy with Him and diligence to follow His instructions. Really, this sums up all growing pains! Success requires time and effort. It is a process. A real, God-breathed, God-driven comeback involves growth and maturity. You are going to have some pain along the way, just like you did growing from a little baby to a full-grown adult. But you kept growing then and you can continue growing now.

Surround yourself with people who understand your growing pains and will help you through them. Immerse yourself in what is true and right. Read and hear and look upon things that will strengthen, not weaken you. Believe what God says about you— because it is true! Then start saying what you believe and changing your world.

5

STAYING STEADY
IN UNSTEADY TIMES

"Okay, I'm starting to feel better and things are beginning to look up for me. The only thing I keep asking is, *What's the point?* The world is going to Hell in a handbasket! I hear a lot of complaining about it, but no one seems to have any answers that make a lasting difference. I don't see how my life can make any difference."

Let's face it. Much of the news you hear today is bad news, and sometimes it's terrifying news. Rarely will the media report an act of heroism or compassion. They are in the business of alarming and discouraging us by reporting the most horrible and grievous events they can find. They are like the town gossip, who roams the streets looking for the most hair-raising story, just so they can be the one to break it to the rest of the town.

When you hear shocking news, it is like a blow to your heart. Blows like these can cause you to feel unsteady, and you need to stay steady to come out of a setback and achieve the comeback God has for you. Whenever I begin to be unnerved and uncertain,

I remember a little girl's words during a life-threatening storm in 1998.

A devastating tornado hit the community in which this girl lived, and she had huddled with her classmates in her elementary school hallway as the funnel cloud roared overhead. Later, a reporter asked her if she had been afraid. She replied matter-of-factly, "No, I just cried and prayed to God." Interestingly enough, no one at her school was injured!

This is an awesome testimony—out of the mouth of a babe—about what it means to stay steady during unsteady or turbulent times. The words of this girl reflected what she believed not what she was experiencing. She was having a setback, but she knew the Author of her comeback! She turned to Jesus, and I don't think it was just a coincidence that no one in her school was hurt.

When life takes on the appearance of a battlefield, you are going to turn to someone or something to remain steady. Built into you is a desire to completely rely on someone or something other than yourself, especially when all hell breaks loose. The question is, who or what will you turn to?

THE RIGHT ENABLER

Today in our culture, there is a lot of talk about addictions of all kinds, and anyone who wants to help a person get free of their addiction should never *enable* them in it. Basically, you don't tell an addict they don't have a problem when it is obvious they do, and you never lie for, substitute for, or take responsibility for them. Otherwise, you will enable them to continue in their problem. You will be their *enabler*. At the same time, if *you* are trying to break free of a terrible habit, co-dependent relationship, or addiction, you need to stay clear of those who enable you in it.

This is very interesting because the word "enabler" now has a totally negative connotation. Yet God designed us to need an enabler to live our lives to the fullest. We cannot do life on our own. The problem is, we tend to turn to other people or chemical substances or a hobby—and end up co-dependent, obsessed, dysfunctional, or addicted to something unhealthy. We do this because we have missed the only Enabler we were created to depend upon.

Let's look at the relationship between Paul and his spiritual son, Timothy. Timothy's mother and grandmother were godly women, but his father was another story. Most of the time Timothy did very well, but every once in awhile he would falter and think about giving up. He needed a mature man to take him in hand, to teach him to stay steady.

When Paul wrote his first letter to Timothy, Timothy was in a setback. There was an economic and spiritual famine in his country, and all hell was coming against his life. In 1 Timothy 1:12-17 Paul said (my paraphrase), "Listen Timothy, Jesus *enabled* me to do what I'm doing now. He saved me, healed me, and now He is doing so many miracles it makes my head swim! He will do the same for you."

I want you to notice that Paul didn't make Timothy dependent upon him. He pointed him to Jesus. Paul could not *enable* Timothy. The kind of enabling he was referring to was supernatural, beyond human ability. He could love Timothy, encourage him, teach him, and be a spiritual father to him; but he could never *enable* him the way God could. Paul was smart enough to know this: If you really want to help someone, point them to Jesus, the right Enabler.

When God enables you, He gives you everything you need to carry out His plan for your life. Everything! No one knew this better than Paul. You can read through the book of Acts and see how God *enabled* him. Everywhere he went to preach the Gospel and teach the Bible, miracles happened. He cast out demons, healed the sick, and led many to faith in Jesus. His ministry was remarkable—one of the greatest comeback stories ever!

Paul was well qualified to tell Timothy, "I know what it's like to feel like giving up, but don't do it! Hold on and keep fighting. Yes, you are young and inexperienced. There is famine in the land, and you feel pressured on all sides; but you've got to take your eyes off the circumstances and realize you don't have to participate in the famine! If you will persevere and keep moving forward, God will *enable* you the same way He enables me. He will give you a feast in your famine."

FEAST ON HIS PROMISES

In the midst of a famine, you need to feast on God's promises. Nothing keeps you steady like the solid rock of God's Word.

The Bible is filled with hundreds of promises that belong to all generations and apply to every aspect of daily living. God promises strength, wisdom, all the fruit of the Spirit (love, joy, peace, patience, kindness, goodness, faithfulness, gentleness and self-control), talents and abilities, success, good marriage and family, protection and security, promotion, guidance, physical well being, and the list goes on and on. Sometimes called blessings or benefits, these promises are available to all who choose to live according to God's principles.

I believe God has specific promises for you that relate directly to His purpose for your life. Whatever your purpose, dream, or vision, there is a promise to meet every need to fulfill it. In 1993, twenty-two-year-old John Foppe was selected as one of the Ten Outstanding Young Americans by the U.S. Junior Chamber of Commerce. John had been born without arms and with a number of serious birth defects. Doctors told his parents he had a one-in-a-million chance to survive, but he overcame the odds. Then they said he would never walk, but at the age of two, John took his first steps.

John shares how, as a child, he bitterly asked God, "Why me?" The response he got was, "John, why not you?" At that point he knew God had a significant purpose for his life, and the promise he held onto was hope for a fulfilling and successful future.

The pain and struggles John endured and overcame seem insurmountable in the natural. Born without arms, he does everything with his feet, including dressing himself, driving a car, writing, cooking, and eating. Through it all, he determined that the only real handicaps are the mental and emotional ones, which prevent us from fully participating in life. In the face of every struggle and setback, John has held onto his promise—a full life—and is now fulfilling his purpose of encouraging and helping others as he speaks to thousands in schools and businesses across America.

Feast on God's promise to you and you will be filled with purpose and joy in the most difficult situations.

The Power of Accepting Responsibility

Back in the '70s, comedian Flip Wilson portrayed a character named Geraldine. No matter what happened, Geraldine's answer was always the same, "The devil made me do it!" This was hilarious because we knew Geraldine did what Geraldine wanted to do, and she caused all her problems. In real-life setbacks, many times the devil didn't have anything to do with our problems either!

Before my good friend Nacho went on to be with the Lord, I had been going to his barber shop to get my hair cut since I was fourteen years old. One day I pulled up in front of his shop and thought I had put my car in park. Actually, I'd put it in reverse. I reached down to get my wallet, and I felt something go *Bam!* I jolted back up in the seat and yelled, "Somebody hit me!" I was mad and got out of my car, looking for the culprit. There was this beat-up, old Celica behind me. Nobody was in it, so I fumed, "This is a hit and run!"

A lady who lived next door to Nacho's came out of her house and said, "I saw it."

I said, "Well, what did he look like?"

She said, "You hit it."

I laughed, "You're teasing."

She said, "No, you hit it."

The owner of the Celica was in the barbershop, so I took a deep breath, went into the shop, and said, "I hit your car." I had to go to my car insurance agent and say, "I hit the car." It was hard to admit I was at fault, but in the end I felt like a man and not a mouse. When our setbacks are caused by our own actions, the quicker we admit responsibility and make things right, the quicker we get to our comeback.

God's supernatural power *enables* you to do the right thing, and when you do the right thing something incredible happens. You become taller, straighter, and *steadier*. Accepting responsibility for your own actions brings stability and consistency to your life. This is what employers are looking for in their employees. It is what a single person is looking for in a mate. And it is what the world around you is waiting to see in someone.

That was my fault. I did it. I said it. I take full responsibility. These are hard statements to utter! They grate against our pride and self-centeredness. They also open the floodgates for God's power to help us stay steady and maintain momentum in a very trying time, whether it is a setback or the process of coming back.

Tenacity

David Letterman does a segment on his show called Stupid Pet Tricks. One night I was watching, and the pet owners brought in a big tree and a pit bull. The trick was that the dog jumped up and ripped the limbs off the tree, one at a time. It was something to see. When the dog got to one big branch that he couldn't rip off, he wouldn't let go. His jaws locked. He growled and ripped and tore at that branch. The audience went wild. That dog did not let go of that branch until he pried it loose.

I marveled at the tenacity of that dog. That was truly holding steady during a very trying time! It is how we need to be in reaching for God's promises and our comeback. We need to latch on and not let go no matter what comes against us. Tenacity means you stay focused and remain fixed; you refuse to get off course. Even when something knocks you to the right or to the left of your path, you just jump back and get on your way again.

Understand this: The battle is always the fiercest just before the victory. Right before your breakthrough, you may feel like anything that could possibly go wrong has gone wrong—all of it at once. That's why you must be prepared to stay steady. Refuse to give up. Like that pit bull, hold on until the last branch breaks loose.

In the midst of all the craziness in this world, don't get distracted by what other people are going through or what they are saying about your life. Have you ever seen a horse in a race wearing blinders on both eyes? That is so it won't get distracted by the horses on either side. That horse focuses on the race and getting across the finish line. Likewise, if you keep your focus on the finish line of your comeback, you won't be knocked off balance and off course by circumstances, by other people, or by anything going on around you. You will hold steady.

Battle Techniques

When you are in a battle, here are four things to do to stay steady:

1. Affirm Yourself and Others. When you are feeling down, start saying something positive to somebody else. Stir them up. Speak life into them. Tell them you are inspired by their life. This is a biblical principle found in 2 Corinthians 1:3-4. It says that when you are in trouble and turn to God for comfort, you will receive further comfort and hold steady by comforting others who are going through the same thing you are going through.

Affirming yourself is a biblical principle. Remember when David and his men came to Ziklag and saw that their families had been kidnapped? This is what it says in 1 Samuel 30:6, in the old *King James Version:* "And David was greatly distressed; for the people spake of stoning him, because the soul of all the people was grieved, every man for his sons and for his daughters: but

David encouraged himself in the LORD his God." In one of his worst battles, David encouraged himself in the Lord. He affirmed himself, and you need to do the same thing.

2. Press Toward the Battle. When you press toward something, you get aggressive. You set your eye on the target and run toward it, not away from it. You want to be on the offensive rather than the defensive because only the offense gets the touchdown! Young David ran *toward* Goliath.

Did you ever wonder why all battle armor was worn on the front of the body? It's because you can't win a battle running away from it. The apostle Paul put it this way, "I press on toward the goal to win the prize for which God has called me" (Philippians 3:14). Paul ran at a steady pace throughout his life, and then he ran right into Heaven. I'm sure Jesus gave him a high five!

3. Reach Higher and Dream Bigger. If one dream dies, believe for a bigger one. If you missed your goal, reach beyond it the next time. When circumstances seem impossible, believe for even more. Set new goals. Listen to people who have accomplished great things in life. If you have a marriage problem, talk to a couple who have been married a lot of years and have a great relationship. Ask them how they have done it. If you got laid off and have a desire to start your own business, talk to successful entrepreneurs who have done what you want to do.

Most important, when you are pushed into a corner, open your heart and mind to the God of all possibilities, and you will be amazed! You will dream yourself out of that corner. Some of my greatest dreams came out of such corners. In the midst of the hard times, setbacks, discouragement, and cheap shots, I saw myself impacting celebrities and professional athletes and encouraging people around the world. God's dreams for us are always much bigger than we could imagine on our own.

4. Pray Big Prayers. Get out of your setback by praying intensely. Get serious with God about all the issues and people in your life. Put pictures of your family members in front of you and pray over them. Pray the kind of "enough-is-enough" prayers that will move the mountains out of their lives. Refuse to cower or step back anymore. The Bible calls the time in which we are living "perilous times," and the battle is fierce.

You can't allow yourself to be lulled into a false sense of security when things are going well, either. You must maintain an aggressive stance in prayer at all times. Charge forward with everything you've got, praying constantly, and you will discover that persistence breaks resistance.

These four things will enable you to hold steady when everyone around you is paralyzed by fear or complacency. God is your enabler! He has put all of His power at your disposal, and you have a right to use His power to get through any and every setback you face. You also have an obligation to clear the way for future generations. Like Paul did for Timothy, you bear the responsibility to leave a legacy of stability and peace in trying times to those who follow you.

Begin to forge that legacy by discovering the promises God has given you in His Word and rehearsing the promises He has whispered to you in your heart. God has said you are going to make it; therefore, you are! As you learn about His benefits, be tenacious. Refuse to let go of them no matter what storms may come. Accept responsibility for your own mistakes, sins, and faults; and do what is right. You will activate all the power of Heaven to go to work for you and keep your head when everyone around you is losing theirs! And that, my friend, is going to impact your world as assuredly as a pebble dropped into a pond causes ripples all the way to shore.

6

YOU WANT ME
TO DO WHAT?

"Well, I'll tell you. Some of the stuff you are asking me to believe and to do sounds crazy. I mean, I'm really trusting you, Sir!"

First of all, what I'm asking you to do is not my idea; it's God's idea. The great thing is that He knows the end from the beginning. Unfortunately, we don't! This is why we call walking with Him an *adventure* in faith. He wants us to follow His instructions to the letter, even when we don't understand them or when we disagree with them. Sometimes what He asks us to do seems impossible; other times it is just plain scary! But no matter how crazy it seems, we need to obey His instructions. In the end, we may find out it was a matter of life or death.

The apostle Paul went from persecuting Christians to becoming a Christian, and in the beginning of his walk with the Lord the Christian community was very wary of him. They knew him as Saul of Tarsus, a zealous Pharisee who had threatened, tortured, or executed many of their friends and family. A man by the name of Ananias certainly knew of Saul, and he was flabbergasted when Jesus appeared to him in a vision and told him to go and pray for Saul.

We don't know much about Ananias. Maybe he was about eighty years of age, in his retirement years, playing golf twice a week. Perhaps he had some favorite TV shows he watched every week, he volunteered at the soup kitchen at his church, and he was a part of the local Promise Keepers. Then along came Jesus and disturbed everything.

Naturally, Ananias tried to talk Him out of it. "'Lord,' Ananias answered, 'I have heard many reports about this man and all the harm he has done to your saints in Jerusalem. And he has come here with authority from the chief priests to arrest all who call on your name'" (Acts 9:13-14).

What did Jesus tell him? "Go! This man is my chosen instrument to carry my name before the Gentiles and their kings and before the people of Israel" (Acts 9:15-16). This tells us something: When Jesus tells you to do something, he doesn't take no for an answer—He says, "Go!"

He also knows the rest of the story. In this case, He knew God had a plan for Saul that was greater than Ananias or anyone else could imagine. He knew that all the zeal Saul had exerted to destroy Christianity was now directed to promote it.

God also had a plan for Ananias, and it was critical that he obey Jesus' instructions no matter how dangerous it appeared to be. I'm sure that years later, as Ananias read the letters Paul wrote and knew that he was reading Holy Scripture, he said to himself, "I'm sure glad I obeyed!" After that, his golfing buddies probably got tired of hearing how he launched the apostle Paul into the ministry!

The truth is, we don't always understand why God has us doing what we are doing, but one thing we do know for certain: He is serious about what He tells us to do, and He always has a good reason.

Prepare for the Unexpected

Like Ananias, you may be going along, minding your own business, and suddenly God will urge you to do something. It may not make any sense, and it may even be dangerous; but if it's His idea, then it must be done. You might as well prepare for the unexpected!

Just think how you would respond if I said to you, "Last week I led Charles Manson to the Lord, and he was baptized. I know he's done some bad things, but he's a changed man. They've let him out of prison, and he's out in the car. He needs a place to stay for a few days. Could you put him up in your guest room?" If you don't know who this guy is, let me tell you. He is certified insane, and in the 1960s, he brutally murdered innocent people. If you look in his eyes, you can see the demons behind them.

Now I have asked you to take this murderer into your home. You would wonder, *Is this for real? Surely God wouldn't want me to endanger my family by taking in a convicted murderer?* Yet, that is just like what God asked Ananias to do. The point is that God's ways are not like our ways, and you can't imagine what He has been dreaming up for you to do in the critical days ahead.

"So how do I prepare for the unexpected? I mean, if I have no idea what God is going to ask me to do, how can I prepare for it? I can't get ready for something that I have no idea is coming and maybe have never seen before."

Getting ready for the unexpected is simple. From the moment you made Jesus your Refuge, He has gently urged you to deal with any character flaws, anything that isn't like Him. Sometimes these are big things, like maybe you were involved in immoral or illegal activities, and you need to turn from these things for good. For all of us, there are "little things" we need to change. Maybe we have lied a lot or have habitually gossiped about other people. Perhaps we have been proud and arrogant. Or maybe we have been so afraid that we have been mean, negative, and grouchy.

God wants to deal with your character, to take care of anything that would hinder you in the big assignments He has for you. Then, when the unexpected comes, your integrity will see you through. There is no way Ananias would have gone to pray for Saul of Tarsus without knowing things between him and Jesus were right. He would not have had the faith or the courage to do it without Jesus by his side.

Being "right" with God means you are trusting and leaning on Him. You must understand something: He is going to lead you through His plan for your life whether you deal with your character flaws or not, so you make the decision whether or not you are going to do life His way or your way. If you do it your way, you may do your assignment, but you might hurt a lot of people along the way—including yourself—because you have refused to properly deal with your issues. If you do it His way, dealing with your issues as they come up, you and everyone around you will have a lot easier time of it. Believe me, I have learned the hard way at times. Don't misunderstand me: You are going to make mistakes no matter how closely you walk with God. All of us do! But when your heart is right with Him, He will supernaturally cover your mistakes and get you through what He's asked you to do in a much easier way.

Raise the Roof

The great thing about Jesus being your Refuge is that He will change you and challenge you—but you know you are safe in Him. It's hard to change, and sometimes it is frightening, but the more you allow Him to change you, the more you see that you really have nothing to fear when you are with Him. He will see you through anything you face, including your own character flaws!

One thing is certain, He is going to stretch you and expand your horizons. You are going to have to raise the roof on your expectations for yourself and life in general in order to think like He thinks and do what He assigns you to do. He's not about maintaining the status quo, saying, "My dad never made more than $20,000 a year so I can't expect anything better." He's about blowing the ceiling off your limited perspective so He can bless you and use you to bless others.

In times like these especially, God is looking for faith to think outside the box and do things differently, if that's what it takes to get the job done. Dare to be different. Break the mold of your past. Take a risk and do something you've never done before.

Have you ever noticed that the same people are blessed with success over and over? Do you know why I believe that is? It is because they have a track record of being willing to raise the roof on their perception, their thinking, and their understanding of who they are and what they are capable of doing. They willingly roll up their sleeves and say, "If God gave me this assignment, He has a way for me to do it. He is the God of all possibilities."

Arnold Schwarzenegger came to Hollywood desiring to be an actor. In fact, he wanted to be an action-adventure star. At first, Arnold only landed roles in movies like *Conan, the Barbarian*, which wasn't a box office blockbuster by any stretch of the imagination.

Critics said it would never happen, besides who's going to remember "Schwarzenegger?" They wanted to change his name to Arnold Strong. They said his jaw was too big, he can't talk correctly, he's muscle-bound. They said he would never make it as a great action-adventure star.

But Arnold had a dream and a plan and it didn't include changing his name. He executed that plan and eventually was paid over $15 million a picture! All this happened because he raised the roof on what he or anyone else thought he was capable of achieving.

Good Ruts and Old Ruts

Part of preparing for any assignment God might give you is establishing good, daily habits. Some ruts are good to get stuck in! It's good to have a time for just you and God, when you can read your Bible, pray and talk to Him, and listen for His response. Your relationship with Him is just like your relationship with anyone else. The only way you can be close to Him is to make the time to get close to Him.

Another good rut to be in is going to church every week, and really becoming a part of a good group of people. This is a good groove to be in because it will challenge you and encourage you to grow and use the gifts and talents God has given you to bless others.

But not all ruts are good. I took my kids to a donut shop one day. As we stood in line waiting to order, the lady behind the counter greeted her regular customers, "Hi Bill, the usual? Morning Dave, the usual? Good to see you Bob, the usual?" She knew exactly what each of them wanted...the usual, the usual, the usual.

I wanted to scream, "Lady, don't you dare give me the usual!"

I don't want the "usual" from life. Do you? I want God to surprise me. I want what He has prepared for me. I can have that if I am flexible enough to shift out of an old rut.

TRANSFORMATION MEANS TRANSITION

If you have walked with Jesus very long, you know He is in the business of transforming you into the person He created you to be. Then, you can do what He has created you to do and enjoy yourself! He's not a slave driver who needs a worker; He's a transformer who wants a whole person to do things with and hang out with. He wants to have fun with you!

Of course, "transformer" means something different in our culture today. We immediately think of blockbuster action movies where robots turn into machines, but the principle is the same. God is transforming us from machine-like beings, who don't have any idea of all the possibilities available to us, into healthy, happy, whole people whose faith in Him rules our lives. Our faith makes it possible for Him to tap us on the shoulder for an amazing assignment. It wasn't that Ananias was so talented or smart; it was that he trusted Jesus.

In order to transform us, Jesus takes us through one transition after another. The Bible has an interesting way of saying this. In 2 Corinthians 3:18 NKJV it says, "But we all, with unveiled face, beholding as in a mirror the glory of the Lord, are being transformed into the same image from glory to glory, just as by the Spirit of the Lord." The Spirit of the Lord is taking us from glory to glory just by our looking at and examining Jesus. We are experiencing one transition after another simply by keeping our eyes on Him.

You Want Me to Do What?

Continually looking at Jesus means you will never remain exactly the same from day to day. I view transition as a passage from one level to the next. Once you pass to the next level, you can never go back to being the way you were on the previous level. Even if you go back to old habits, you will not be the same inside because you have experienced something better. Transition makes a permanent mark on the inside of you, so that whatever you are doing on the outside is affected.

Most of us don't want to move and shift in transition. It may seem too much, too overwhelming, because transition causes us to change, to be inconvenienced, disturbed, bothered, and stretched. We may even feel like putting a "do not disturb" sign on our door, but God has a way of drawing us out!

The New York Times reporter, Henry Stanley, was sent to Africa to find the famous medical doctor/missionary, Dr. Livingston, and bring him back to civilization. Dr. Livingston had lost touch with the outside world and many believed he was dead. Always seeking a news scoop, Stanley trekked through the mountains and valleys of unexplored Africa for a year. He was attacked and chased by cannibals, his caravan was plagued by sickness and man-eating lions, and there was no clue as to the whereabouts of Dr. Livingston.

Stanley became weary and sick with fever, then a group of African tribesmen wandered into his camp and spoke of a white doctor. He went with them and found the elderly Dr. Livingston healing the sick, teaching the Gospel, and single-handedly exploring and mapping the vast interior of Africa.

Dr. Livingston had a vision to explore and map Africa so that Europeans would no longer fear it. He wanted to open up Africa to the world. Stanley proceeded to accompany him on some of the mapping expeditions and was deeply impacted by Dr. Livingston's faith and purpose. He was transformed simply by looking at this remarkable man day after day, and he unconsciously caught the doctor's vision as a result.

That is the way it is with you and Jesus. The more you look at Him, the more time you spend with Him, the more of your life you surrender to Him, the more you will go "from glory to glory." You will become like Him and you will catch His vision for your life, just like Stanley caught Dr. Livington's. He not only saw Dr. Livingston; he saw Jesus in Dr. Livingston.

When Henry Stanley went back to England, those who had known him saw that he was a transformed man because of his time with Dr. Livingston. After a few years of walking with Jesus, your old friends will probably be saying, "Can you believe the difference? What's being accomplished is amazing. It's really a miracle, you know."

FAITH AND WILLINGNESS

God uses ordinary people like you and me to do things that don't make sense. They don't make sense to us or anyone around us because we can't see the end from the beginning like He does. He knew there was going to be a flood when He told Noah to build the ark. He knew what Jesus was going to do for the human race when He told Mary she would have a child that was not fathered by Joseph but by Him. Noah's and Mary's faith and willingness to carry out God's plan for their lives changed the world, but they really didn't know what they were doing!

Ananias was also a willing, faith-ruled person. God didn't choose him because he was highly educated—although he may have been. The qualifications for doing something world-changing for God are simply faith and willingness. Faith means trusting God to do the impossible as you step into an arena you know little to nothing about. Willingness is also based on faith and trust in God. Because He is a loving Father and has given you eternal life and peace, you are willing to put your life on the line for Him.

Faith and willingness make room for bigger and better things in your life. They open the doors for God to surprise you with something new. You may be thinking, *But I'm having trouble with the little things in my life. How can I handle anything bigger? I'm in a setback, for Pete's sake!* As you trust God for the little things, the big things will unfold.

The God idea for your life may be so big that it would overwhelm you if He revealed every detail at one time. That is why He takes you through one transition after another. As you are transformed and take one step at a time, the plan will unfold. There will still be times of feeling overwhelmed, ill equipped, and totally unqualified; but that is where His supernatural power comes in to see you through. How does His supernatural power come in? Through your faith and willingness!

The supernatural power of the Holy Spirit was in Ananias and upon Ananias when he visited Saul of Tarsus. Divine courage and strength were in him to get him there, and divine healing power was on him to pray for Saul's eyes to be healed. Ananias' faith and willingness brought God's miraculous power into his assignment.

THE DIVINE SETUP

It is God's job to guide you, guard you, and govern you. No one demonstrated that more than former heavyweight boxer, George Foreman. George used to be a very disturbed, angry individual. Then one day Jesus appeared to him in a very real way, just like He did Ananias. George had just lost a fight, and he was lying in the back room on a table when Jesus appeared and George was ultimately rescued by the grace of God.

George gave his life to Jesus Christ, got involved in God's process of transformation through transition, and began to see God's comeback plan for him.[2] The happy, smiling face you now see on TV is not the same man George Foreman was before he made Jesus his Refuge. Now he is selling George Foreman Grills by the thousands and enjoying all those kids who are also named George!

Back in the time when Jesus was on the Earth, there was another man like George. He was a fisherman who had fished all night and caught nothing. He was probably feeling sorry for himself when Jesus came along and asked him if He could stand in his boat to preach to a bunch of people on the shore. The fisherman shrugged his shoulders and said, "Sure. It's not doing me any good. Might as well do you some good."

After Jesus finished preaching, He told the fisherman to take his boats back out, cast all his nets, and he would get a big catch of fish. Now you must understand what He was asking this guy to do. Fishing is always better at night, and the fisherman had thrown his nets last night in the place Jesus was telling him to throw them. There was no reason for him to believe that what Jesus was proposing would work.

For some reason, the fisherman did what Jesus told him to do, except he didn't cast all his nets. He just threw out one net. Fish began to jump into that net until it was breaking apart, and that is when the fisherman's proud and hard heart also broke. Read the story in Luke, chapter 5, where Peter falls at Jesus' feet and says, "Go away from me, Lord; I am a sinful man!" (v.8).

Jesus saw Peter's change of heart. He knew Peter had faith and willingness, so He gave him the assignment that would change his life forever: "Don't be afraid; from now on you will catch men" (v.10). Now Peter knew how to catch fish, but catching people was another matter! Nevertheless, he had seen a miracle catch of fish, so he had faith Jesus would enable him to bring in a miracle catch of people.

People who don't throw their nets into the deep cling to their preconceived ideas of how their life should be, and their own rigid thinking locks them into mediocrity. Peter broke out of the old rut he was in and once he did it, he never looked back.

The divine setup is that when we cooperate with God's comeback plan by stepping out in faith to do what looks impossible, His supernatural ability will enable us to perform miracles. Peter's setback was having no fish to show after a full night's work. He was discouraged and disgruntled. Then Jesus offered him an assignment that appeared ridiculous. When Peter decided to trust Him and obey, he got his comeback catch—and it was more than he could handle!

When God sets you up for a miracle, it will always be beyond what you can think or imagine.

DIVINE FAVOR

When Ananias went to pray for Saul of Tarsus, he didn't go alone. When Jesus sends you, He goes with you; and if He is with you then you have His favor on your life. He puts favor on your person, your path, and your efforts. There are times when divine favor just falls on you. It's like your forehead is stamped "special," and no matter where you go or what you do, things just work out. You can look at the life of Jesus and see divine favor on Him.

Sometimes favor falls on a specific path and when you follow it, miracles happen. God told Jonah to preach to the Ninevites (read all about it in the book of Jonah). He had a path or journey for Jonah to do this assignment, but Jonah did not want to go. Because of his disobedience, his path included Shamu University—the belly of a whale! That's how far God will go to get you back on His path, which is always much smoother! Once Jonah surrendered and went God's way, which was to Nineveh, the whole place repented and came back to the Lord. Miracles happen on God's pathway!

Finally, favor falls on your efforts. God waits for us to toss that net into the deep before He gives us the miracle catch. When my daughter Chloe was small and wanted to get out of her crib, she would start throwing things out onto the floor. Then she would shake the rails, and scream, "Get me outta here!!!" We were trying to get her to go to sleep, so we just ignored her. It really shocked us when one night she shook the crib rails with all her might and hollered, "Get me outta here! I know you can hear me!!!!" That night her efforts found favor with her parents!

God's favor means you will have a supernatural acceptance, approval, and connection with the people you meet in your assignment. Even those who dislike you and try to trip you up will see it. It also means that everything you do will prosper, and all the natural things you encounter will cooperate with you—if you are doing God's will.

Peter had favor with the sea and the fish when he threw his net out into the deep because he was doing what Jesus told him to do. Even natural things line up and cooperate when you are doing the assignment He has given you. This is how I can say to you that your comeback is just waiting for you, and it is a done deal. As soon as you begin to take those steps of transition and transformation, as soon as you step out in faith and are willing, you will be on your way to obtaining your miracle comeback.

Maybe you feel like Chloe did back then. In the midst of your setback, you are screaming, "Get me out of here!" But take a moment to stop struggling against the situation you are in and ask yourself a few questions. Am I fighting to hold onto a God-given promise, or am I just fighting to get my way? Do I want out of this situation because it's unscriptural or do I want out merely because it's uncomfortable? Am I truly seeking God's will or my way? Take some time to uncover your real motivation. You may be surprised to discover that you're bucking against God—and that's a bad place to be.

The one thing to remember when God asks you to leave your comfort zone and do something that looks impossible, ridiculous, or outrageous is that He puts his favor on you when you are in sync with Him. He can't bless you or move supernaturally when you are doing things your way or going against His will. He can only help you and bless you beyond your wildest dreams if you are walking with Him.

The comeback He has prepared for you may be a process of transitions and transformation that is far different from the way you thought it would be or wanted it to be, but I can tell you by experience and by the truth of His Word that it is the best comeback for you. The next time He asks you to do something and your initial reaction is, "You want me to do what?!!!" trust Him, walk with Him—and then watch His divine favor turn your life into a miraculous adventure.

7

MASTERPIECE IN MOTION

"Okay, I have reached an impasse. It's like I've hit a wall and nothing I do is working. What's going on?"

I have a good friend who struggled with his career in the early 1970s. He was working as a talent agent in Los Angeles and wasn't having much success. To ease the stress of his situation, he would do something he had loved to do since he was a kid: bake chocolate chip cookies. While baking cookies one day, he had an idea. Why not send cookies to celebrities to try and get a meeting with them?

The cookies were such a success that his clients began urging him to open his own store, which eventually he did. On March 10, 1975, Wally Amos opened a cookie store on Sunset Boulevard, and the name was *Famous Amos*. *Famous Amos* cookies can now be found in almost every supermarket around the nation, not to mention many places worldwide.[1]

Sending cookies to celebrities was a little thing, and some people might call it a stupid idea; but it worked for Wally Amos! He knew that what he had done up to that point had not worked, and he had nothing to lose. That is when God can really get through to us—when we have nothing to lose and we are open to all possibilities.

During a setback, you can be a masterpiece in motion.

Your inner cry for more becomes more pronounced during a setback, but it is not some random cry. We all want more, but the increase we must be seeking is always connected to our divine purpose. God created each one of us with a heart that yearns to fulfill our purpose in life. Some fulfill their purpose by raising children and helping raise other people's children. Others build beautiful homes and buildings. Some discover important new inventions, while others paint portraits that seem alive. Whatever your purpose is, if you haven't walked into it, it's begging to come out.

What you need in a setback is revelation. Revelation is when the light bulb goes on in your head and the fires of passion are lit in your heart. All of a sudden, you understand something you have never understood before, and you understand it on a very deep level. You have finally seen God's fingerprint in your DNA. You know His purpose for your life.

Revelation is not taught; it is supernaturally imparted. It is not an intellectual understanding; it is a heart/spirit understanding. I can teach you that studying the Bible is like daily nourishment for the spirit and soul, but the depth of my revelation cannot be taught. You must catch that revelation for yourself. You have to hear it for yourself from God, deep inside you.

I can look at you and God may give me a revelation of what your purpose is. I can tell you your purpose and even teach you all about that purpose. But all of this comes to nothing if you do not have a revelation of your purpose directly from God. If you don't hear it from Him, all you will be doing is living out what I told you. Now I'm fairly accurate in prophesying to people, but I'm not perfect. I can make a mistake. God never will. That's one reason you need to hear it from Him.

Another reason you need to hear your purpose from Him is because something supernatural happens inside you when He declares your purpose inside you. He lights a divine fire in your heart that will move you forward and give you momentum for a lifetime. This is a fire that can burn up character flaws, burn through setbacks, and ignite your comeback. It's a fire that will illuminate the path God has forged for you and give you the faith and perseverance to walk it out.

If you don't know what your purpose is, you can be confident that God wants to reveal it to you. He will reveal it to you as you spend time with Him. And get ready, because you can't accomplish it on your own! You need His wisdom on how to accomplish it and the timing of certain aspects of it, and you need His supernatural provision and protection.

"But what about all these famous, wealthy people who obviously are fulfilling their purpose and don't know Jesus or even believe in God? How does that happen?"

It's true. Some know their purpose and do not know or serve the God who gave them that purpose; but the Bible has something interesting to say about that. The God who made us says that when we attempt our purpose apart from Him, the riches we make come with sorrow (Proverbs 10:22), and the things we accomplish are all done in vain (Ecclesiastes 12). At the end of our lives, there is a hollow cavity in the center of our being that knows we missed the most important part of living: knowing God.

Apart from God, you are going to be frustrated big time. Yes, you are a masterpiece in motion—but you are His masterpiece. You are His idea, His treasure, and only He can unlock the great gift to the world that you are.

Shaped As Seems Best

This is the word that came to Jeremiah from the LORD: "Go down to the potter's house, and there I will give you my message." So I went down to the potter's house, and I saw him working at the wheel. But the pot he was shaping from the clay was marred in his hands; so the potter formed it into another pot, shaping it as seemed best to him.

Then the word of the LORD came to me: "O house of Israel, can I not do with you as this potter does?" declares the LORD. "Like clay in the hand of the potter, so are you in my hand, O house of Israel.

This quote from the Bible is found in Jeremiah 18:1-6. God told the prophet Jeremiah to watch how a potter works the clay, and Jeremiah noticed that the potter formed a marred pot into another pot, "as seemed best to him." This is a powerful phrase, and it is just what we are talking about. You have an idea of what your life should be like, but God's idea is so much better. So rather than let you create your own marred life, He wants to show you the great plan He has for you—shaping your life as seems best to Him. He's the potter; you are the clay.

I was walking through the supermarket one day, and I saw a little kid fighting with his mother. He wanted sweets, and she didn't think he should have them. After seeing how hyper he was, I didn't either! The mother was pushing the cart, and her son would wait until she turned her back to grab the Sugar Smacks and put them under the cart. Unfortunately for him, God blessed mothers with sixteen eyes all over their head. Nothing gets by them. She just simply stopped, took the Sugar Smacks out of the cart, and put them back.

Was that kid mad! He never gave up. Aisle after aisle he kept trying this trick, and one of those sixteen eyes caught it every time. Finally, he went for some type of Hostess product, grabbed it, and put it under the cart. She said, "All right. Now I've had it. I'm going to spank you." And she did it, smack on the bottom. He threw both arms up in the air, planted his hands on his hips and looked at her as though to say, "What's the big idea? Why'd you do that?"

That is exactly how we act in life sometimes. God knows what is best for us, and when He disciplines us like a good Father we turn around and say, "What's the big idea? I wanted to marry that man! So what if He only took a bath once a month and chewed and spit. I could have cleaned him up!" Thank the Lord He is shaping us as seems best to Him and not to us!

DEFAULT OR DESIGN?

Don't fight the plan of God or you will live by default instead of design. Let me explain exactly what I mean by that. When you are working on the computer, there are certain "defaults" built in. These are things that will automatically type or happen if you don't override them by your "design." For example, in Microsoft Word software, if you start numbering a series of points in your essay, the computer program will automatically format those numbered points as bullets, which are indented and set a certain way. If you do not want this to happen, you must override "auto format" and type in your own design for your numbered points.

God is the Great Creator and Master Designer. If you want to be truly creative and inventive and have a great adventure discovering who you are and how to fulfill your purpose, you need to follow His design. If you go off on your own, you will experience the defaults of life. The defaults of life are not God's best plan, but He set them in place. They are to remind you that there is a better way to live your life.

Life without divine purpose is just an experiment. If you don't live by God's design, as seems best to Him, you probably will be like a cat constantly chasing its tail, always moving but getting nowhere and accomplishing nothing. If you do catch your tail, you will not know why you did it or what to do with it!

"Sometimes I'm not sure if I'm in God's design or defaulting on everything. How can you be sure?"

Our Instruction Manual says it this way, "You will go out in joy and be led forth in peace" (Isaiah 55:12). You will be led, or make all your decisions, based on inner peace. When that peace that you just can't put into words is within you, you know you are doing the right thing. On the other hand, when your spirit is grieved or even a little bit unsettled, you know either you are not doing the right thing or it is not the right time to do it.

This verse also says that you will go out in joy, and we know that "the joy of the LORD is your strength" (Nehemiah 8:10). When you have total peace, even if you are embarking on something that is dangerous, you will have God's strength. Biblical joy is not always "happy, happy" and whistling and singing your way through life! Sometimes the joy of the Lord is the supernatural strength and courage to do the difficult or life-threatening thing you know you have to do.

Even if there are still obstacles to overcome along the way, you will have a peace and a joy to your life because you know you are smack dab in the middle of God's design for your life. And if you fall into default mode, you will have an uneasiness and discomfort inside that will alert you to the fact that you have veered off the path God has set for you. You see, God even designed the default to lovingly guide you to where you need to go!

GOD'S PROCESS

I was so into this biblical concept of God being the potter and me being the clay, I decided to visit a shop and watch a potter work. I discovered that although each potter has a different style that makes their pots unique, each one follows a similar, basic process. Before we go through the steps in this process, however, there is something very important you need to know.

The only way you are going to get through many parts of the process of becoming God's masterpiece is to understand in depth what Jesus did for you. If you know the weight of what He did *for you,* then you will be able to do what He asks you to do *for Him.* You will go through the hard parts of the Potter's process with gratitude rather than bitterness.

Jesus was rejected, insulted, mocked, spit upon, beaten up, scourged (whipped with leather strips that had pieces of metal and glass embedded in them), crowned with long, sharp thorns, nailed to a cross, and forsaken by all but a few—for you. He died, saying, "Father, forgive them. They have no idea what they are doing." He wasn't only talking about the people who had done all these terrible things to Him; He was talking about you. You have no idea what you are doing apart from God.

Our sins brought Jesus to the cross, and His cross accomplished something that no other cross did—He paid the debt for my sins and your sins. In all that pain and suffering, He forgave you and me. He was humble and loving. Now He is asking you to become like Him, to endure hardship and to be humbled. To show His love and forgiveness to others the way He has shown it to you.

Come down off your high horse and do a good job for the rude, harsh employer God led you to serve. Bake a casserole for your sick neighbor who never has a good word for you or your family. Forgive everyone who does anything to offend you just as Jesus forgave you—that is the key to getting through the Potter's process. So here we go!

1. The potter digs the clay out of the ground. This is such a great picture of being born again spiritually. The Father reaches into the kingdom of darkness, gathers us up in all our selfishness and sin, forgives us, and places us in His kingdom of light and love to be molded and formed into His masterpiece.

2. The potter soaks the clay in water to make it pliable and flexible. What does God do when He saves us? He immediately begins to soak us in His truth and love so He can transform us and mold us into who He created us to be. This is a sweet time for most believers. Some call it the honeymoon period. The Father is laying a foundation of love and truth that will stand through all the storms ahead of us.

3. When the clay is ready, the potter begins to smite it and work it. I'm convinced this is like good coaching. Like a coach, God brings discipline into our lives for our own good. I'm sure you would agree that to have a championship team, you must first have a championship coach!

God is in the business of getting you and keeping you in shape inside and out—and He does that through the authorities He brings into your life. Sometimes you don't like that. You feel like those He wants you to serve are unjust, unfair, and often unworthy to lead you and guide you. But a good coach will use authority to teach you what you need to learn, like patience, faithfulness, honesty, and how to control your mouth. So the next time you are having problems with someone at work, consider the possibility that it may be God trying to build His character in you.

4. After the potter smites and works the clay, he pushes a thin wire into it. By this time the clay is just a big lump, but it has been through a lot. It thinks it's a big shot because it has been smacked and kneaded. It has dumped some old ideas and embraced some truth, and it is a lot more knowledgeable and flexible. It thinks it has arrived. It has not.

As the potter began to push a thin wire into the clay, I asked him, "Why are you doing that?"

He replied, "Because when I put the pot in the furnace, if I don't get out every air bubble, the pot will crack or explode."

Isn't that just like God, prodding and poking our imperfections? He knows that if we don't become people of integrity, disciplined and committed, we are going to crack and explode when things get tough. He is trying to transform us inside, to purify our thoughts and break open every air pocket of immorality or stinginess or self-promotion. He knows that these are the inner weaknesses that can come to the surface and tear our lives apart as we achieve our purpose—or abort our purpose altogether.

When He pushes His wire of truth into your inner being, He will poke every area of your life. His Word will challenge you about gossip, about your physical fitness, about racism and prejudice, about being a complainer, about bad habits and addictions, and certainly about anything immoral or illegal that you have been into. This will reveal your level of commitment to the Lord and His plan for your life.

Too many of us run for the sprint, thinking we can get away with one great victory that will last a lifetime. We conquer one area of our lives and think we have arrived. But God designed life as a marathon. He is into long-distance running that covers every mile of the track in His design. It takes commitment and endurance to run His race well!

When I was nineteen, I decided to serve God. I talked with one of my sisters about my decision, and she asked, "What type of Christian do you want to be? What type of leader do you want to be? Do you want to train for the high school team or for the Olympics?"

I said, "What do you mean?"

She said, "I knew a girl who won a silver medal in the Olympics. She had to give it her life. At five in the morning, six days a week, while other people were sleeping, she was swimming. So if you want to train for the Olympics in the realm of the Spirit, you're going to have to give it your life."

I chose to give it my life, and I have never regretted it. However, there have been times when God's poking and prodding were really unpleasant, because He was exposing all the faults and weaknesses I was trying to hide! The more I yielded to Him, the better I got.

5. **After being struck, worked, prodded, and poked, the potter puts the clay on the wheel.** Now the potter begins to shape the clay. He puts it on his potter's wheel and begins to turn the wheel. He adds more water as needed and molds the clay with his hands as it turns. He is smoothing the rough edges as he brings forth its shape and form.

As our Potter begins turning us on His wheel, revealing all our gifts and talents, we say, "Look at me! I'm really something!" The angels probably have their arms crossed and are shaking their heads, "That's one of the biggest lumps we've ever seen!"

Our Potter molds us with His hands, urging us to come in line with His design for our life. Every now and then we feel a pinch here or a nudge there. "Ouch!" We don't like that, do we? But nothing good happens without self-discipline. Some people want to own their own company, but they can't keep their car clean. The Potter teaches them that the discipline they gain in keeping their car clean will be the discipline that sees them through hard economic times in their business.

6. **The potter sets the pot on a shelf to harden.** This is where we get tough in a good way or a bad way. During times of being

rejected, unnoticed, unsuccessful, or simply being set aside, we will either become bitter or better. This is what I call the John the Baptist phase of the process. When Jesus came on the scene, John was the famous one. No one knew Jesus, but they all had heard of John. He was the rock star of the desert! Suddenly Jesus showed up, and John said, "He must increase, but I must decrease" (John 3:30 NKJV). John could say this because he understood the weight of what Jesus was about to do for him and for the world.

You have always been the center of your world up to this time. Even when you got saved it was all about you—what you were doing for God, what God was doing for you. Now you are on the shelf. There is nobody around to boast to, nobody wants to hear what's going on with you except a few diehard friends, and the Potter seems to have turned His back on you. That's because He wants you to see what is most important. He is forming Jesus in you. It's not about you anymore. You must decrease so He can increase.

You are on the shelf flipping burgers, when you want to be a chef in a five-star restaurant. You are on the shelf in debt, when you know you belong on Wall Street doing big deals. You are on the shelf single, when you know you should be married, have two children, and a dog named Ralph. The Potter has presented you with a choice. You can become bitter about this turn of events, or you can become humble and obedient like Jesus.

Shelf time is a waiting period, and waiting is a necessary part of God's process. Moses spent forty years on the backside of the desert before he came to lead the children of Israel out of Egypt

(Acts 7:23-30). The apostle Paul spent fourteen years in the wilderness getting Saul out of Paul (Galatians 1:17,2:1) before He was fully received by the church in Jerusalem. All world-changers go through shelf time, even Jesus. He didn't begin his ministry on Earth until he was thirty years old (Luke 3:23).

We do strange things on the shelf. We get lonely and cry, "Yoo-hoo! God! Did you forget about me? Doesn't anybody know I'm here?"

We get frustrated and complain, "I don't know why I have to stay here. I already know how to flip burgers. I've done it a million times. This isn't fair. When is God going to use my gifts and talents to the fullest?"

We get jealous of anyone else who seems to be moving on with their lives, saying, "I don't know why she got that promotion. Everybody knows I have more experience than she does. Who did she brown nose?"

Sometimes we hop off the shelf only to go back on it because we haven't learned the patience, perseverance, and humility we needed to learn. The Potter puts the pot on the shelf for a reason, and only He knows when it is ready to be taken down; so don't take yourself down!

When are you finished with the shelf test? When the humility and compassion of Jesus have been formed in you. You are yielded and open. You will serve God anywhere and do anything for Him. If He wants you to feed hungry children in Appalachia instead of being a chef in a five-star restaurant, you will do it. When someone needs help you say, "I will help you. Tell me what to do." You're finished with the shelf test when all the kicking and screaming has left you, and you have learned to overcome your pride and self-centeredness.

When Jesus is formed in you, you are ready for your comeback.

7. The potter takes the pot off the shelf and glazes it. When you realize it is all about Jesus and not about you, God takes you off the shelf and then on to places you could never have gotten to on your own. Networking, motivational seminars, designer clothes, and a makeover will never take you to these places. Suddenly you find yourself owning your own franchise, president of the company, living in a big, new house. Inside you know the truth: God did this. You were incapable of putting this glaze on yourself. You also know that the glaze is not in what you do or what you have; the glaze is His glory. It is His anointing and favor resting upon your life. It His character and power coming through a yielded vessel who loves the Potter more than life.

What you are about to find out is that the Potter puts that glaze on the pot for a reason: the pot must be glazed to shine through the fire of the kiln. You are about to go to war like never before, and you need the shield of faith to get through it. Everything the Potter has done up to now has been to prepare you for the fire, so that you can endure it, get the full benefit of it, and come out more beautiful and more resilient than ever before.

8. The potter puts the pot in the kiln to be fired. A kiln is an extremely hot furnace. Your kiln is a battlefield of fire. You have to deal with all kinds of crazy people and horrendous situations. Now you understand that the authorities and coaches and teachers you had through the years weren't as unjust, unfair, and unworthy as you thought! You have stepped into their shoes, and the view is quite different from where you were before. The responsibilities are greater, the losses are more devastating, and the lives of more than just you are on the line.

It's like a championship boxing match. You have had fights before, but never against this great of an opponent. You have trained, you have studied your adversary, but now it's time to get in the ring and see what you are made of. There you are, standing face-to-face with the enemy, and you feel frightened and alone. But if you glance back at your corner, you will see your number-one supporter, your Cornerman.

In boxing, the cornerman is the fighter's coach. He stays outside the combat area during the fight, but is always close by so he can instruct and encourage his fighter. That's how Jesus handles us when we are in the "furnace." He assists us from the side, telling us, "Don't quit! You can do it! Punch him here. Hit him there! You didn't train this hard to be beaten!"

In the fires of life you find out why you needed the glaze of God! The higher the call, the hotter the fire. If you have submitted to the Potter every step of the way, you may be overwhelmed by the fire you are facing, but you will not be overcome by it! You know who prepared you, and He is right there with you. He made you and He will sustain you in everything He has called you to do. I like how *The Message* puts it in Ephesians 2:7-10:

> *Now God has us where he wants us, with all the time in this world and the next to shower grace and kindness upon us in Christ Jesus. Saving is all his idea, and all his work. All we do is trust him enough to let him do it. It's God's gift from start to finish! We don't play the major role. If we did, we'd probably go around bragging that we'd done the whole thing! No, we neither make nor save ourselves. God does both the making and saving. He creates each of us by Christ Jesus to join him in the work he does, the good work he has gotten ready for us to do, work we had better be doing.*

9. The potter removes the pot from the kiln and allows it to cool. There may be several glazes and several trips to the kiln before the pot has the strength and shine to satisfy the potter, and anyone who has loved and served God for long knows that there is more than one battle to fight, more than one setback to struggle through, and more than one comeback. That is why you are a masterpiece *in motion.* You will not stop learning, growing, and accomplishing what the Master Potter has destined for you to accomplish until you leave this life and walk right into Heaven.

10. The potter puts the pot on display. The potter knows when the pot is ready to be admired, respected, and sought after—or criticized and not appreciated because it is so unique! Likewise, God knows when you will be able to handle the criticism *and* praise of people, the whispers of the enemy that you are so great or so worthless, and the temptation to believe everything you hear!

You will find that if you submitted to God's process in your setback, when you come back you will be filled with Him instead of yourself. This means you will keep your head and heart in the right place whether people are for you or against you. You know Who made you and Who sustains you. You are God's work of art, created to do the good works He designed for you to do.

The Potter alone knows the great value and worth of his masterpiece.

At this point in the process you still are not perfect, but you are a lot better! Through setbacks and comebacks, you have developed a deeper, more intimate relationship with God. His Word is alive in you and His Spirit shines brightly through you. Praying, hearing His instructions, and obeying His instructions are now a way of life.

There are still times of confronting your pride and self-centeredness, of putting down and overcoming old habits and wrong thinking, but you are now fully fired and glazed. You are what the Bible calls a vessel of honor, one who bears the character and power of Jesus in everything you do. You are not too proud to admit when you mess up or are wrong. When people compliment and praise you, you remain humble and don't get the big head; and when you are criticized you, humbly take it to the Lord. He may change you, but He will not crush you; and He will always affirm you.

God knows what it is going to take to get the greatest results. He sees your past, your present, and your future. He has a remarkable design for your life and all you need to do is submit to His gentle hands. It is at that moment you become His masterpiece in motion.

8

LEAVING A LEGACY

"**W**hy is getting up and moving through a setback so hard? I'm trying to do everything I have been reading in this book, but it seems like for every step I take forward I get shoved back about five steps. It's frustrating, and sometimes I wonder if it's worth it."

There is a very good reason why you are in the heat of a battle for your comeback. It's not just about you.

"Right, I know. It's about God's plan of changing lives."

That's true, and I'm glad you know that now! But there is more. It is also about what you carry in you. You carry generations of people who will serve the Lord and kick the enemy out of families, communities, and even nations. There is a lot at stake here. There are generations at stake. The children you have naturally and the children you influence spiritually will carry your vision for rising up from any setback to obtain a comeback—and that means the enemy can't stop you or generations to come!

RAISING UP CHAMPIONS

If my mother had given up as she was raising five children on her own, she would have put a "give up" spirit in all of her children. If your children see you giving up in the midst of a setback, they will adopt a spirit of failure instead of a spirit of overcoming adversity. On the other hand, if they see you fight through every obstacle and difficulty, you will train a generation of champions who will say, "My father didn't give up, my mother didn't give up, and I won't either."

It's up to our generation to be a positive example and to encourage the next generation. God wants our young people to be an example during their youth in areas of life where we missed it. Our children don't have to have drinking problems. They don't have to go through divorce or live defeated lives. You can be the one to stir them up, shake them up, and tell them there is a champion inside of them just waiting to come out. Tell them God has a plan for their lives, and they are destined to do greater things than we ever thought of doing.

"Well, what about me? No one in my family ever amounted to anything. I never saw my daddy or my mama get up from anything but a hangover, and then they just went out and got high again."

You can still make it! You can decide to be the role model and reverse your whole generational pattern from a bad one to a good one. Some people just need to be encouraged, and I'm encouraging you right now. Some of the greatest men and women in the Bible just needed encouragement to do incredible things and change history. For example, God sent a woman named Deborah to help a man named Barak fulfill his destiny (Judges 4-5). Barak's name means lightning—swift, dynamic, and powerful—but he was acting the complete opposite. He was scared of his own shadow.

Deborah came to him and said, "Barak, God wants you to defeat the Canaanite army."

Barak said, "I don't think so. I'm afraid." In all fairness, Barak had a reason to be afraid. The Canaanites loved to cut folks' arms and legs off and then burn them alive!

Deborah said, "Don't worry; God's going to be with you, and He has given me His surefire plan to defeat the enemy."

Barak said, "I don't care. I'm just not into this at all."

Deborah kept coming, "Then why did God tell me to come get you? Don't you see that He made you to do this? Have a little faith, Barak! God wouldn't ask you to do this if He didn't intend on seeing you through it. It's time you got out there and found out just who you are and who God is."

Barak said, "Well, if you'll go with me, I'll go." Obviously he hadn't heard of male chauvinism—or else he didn't think she would be stupid enough to actually go along!

Deborah could have said, "What a loser," and walked away; but she saw Barak through God's eyes. She saw him as a history-maker. That's the way we need to see our children and grandchildren, especially when they say and do stupid things! Who knows what their destiny may be. We may have another Billy Graham or Dr. Schweitzer living in our house.

Deborah and Barak gathered an army and then walked five miles to fight the Canaanite army. I can just imagine what that journey was like. She was a classy woman, dressed in her designer dress and shoes. She's got her Gucci bag over her shoulder and a donkey carrying her Louis Vuitton luggage. The first mile, she breaks a heel off her shoe. By the second mile, her hair has lost its bounce and she's wondering what she's doing with a guy who has no idea who he is.

There was something Deborah knew that no one else might have known, however, and it made all her struggles with Barak worth it. She knew what God could do in someone's life if they let Him, and she knew what God wanted to do with the Canaanites! All she and Barak had to do was follow God's plan, and not only would they save their neighborhood, but also they would free the whole nation of Israel from the Canaanites' harsh rule.

At the end of this five-mile journey, a miracle happened. Barak suddenly got fired up, he and the Israelite army attacked the Canaanites, and they totally whipped them! He became a champion and was even written up in the "Who's Who of Faith" in the eleventh chapter of Hebrews, verse 32.

THE POWER OF YOUR WORDS

You ask, "What did that woman say to that man? I mean, five miles was a long journey in those days, and you know she must have bent his ear!"

I believe every step of the way, Deborah bombarded Barak with life-changing words that built up his faith in God and God's ability to use him. Her conversation went something like this. "C'mon, you weren't called lightning for nothing! Don't you know God told your daddy and mama to name you that? With the Most High God backing you, you cannot lose! Act like the champion you are! Stir yourself up! Wake yourself up! Do what God called you to do! I know that all you need to do is have faith in God, and you've got what it takes to do what He says!"

Like Barak in the Bible, many people are just one conversation away from greatness. Here is a great poem that illustrates this truth.

If a child lives with criticism, he learns to condemn.

If a child lives with hostility, he learns to fight.

If a child lives with ridicule, he learns to be shy.

If a child lives with shame, he learns to feel guilty.

If a child lives with tolerance, he learns to be patient.

If a child lives with encouragement, he learns confidence.

If a child lives with praise, he learns to appreciate.

If a child lives with fairness, he learns justice.

If a child lives with security, he learns to have faith.

If a child lives with approval, he learns to like himself.

If a child lives with acceptance and friendship,

He learns to find love in the world.

—Amanda Cater[1]

What words do our children or grandchildren hear? Our young people can have more confidence and sustained momentum if we help them up, stir them up, and tell them they can make it. We can raise them up knowing that God loves them, that He has a great plan for their lives, and He will enable them to fulfill it.

I did some research on people who did great things at a young age. Alexander the Great conquered the world at twenty-three. Charles Dickens wrote *The Pickwick Papers* at twenty-four and the classic *Oliver Twist* at twenty-five. Francis of Assisi was twenty-five when he founded the Franciscan order. Billy Graham was thirty-one when he preached the Los Angeles crusade that shook the city and launched his international ministry.

I believe God has destined some of our children to do great things early in their lives, and we need to be praying for our kids. He wants us to begin raising up generation after generation of youth who have a passion for their purpose and the God who gave them their purpose. Instead of blaming someone or something else for their setbacks and expecting a handout, they will reach for the Refuge and get a hand up!

Those who believe the promises of God, who submit themselves to the Master Potter, who are determined to leave a legacy for the next generation, won't strike out or sit out—and neither will their children and their children's children. They will know the power of their words, and they will be a walking encouragement to everyone they know. They will reach out one more time to those who have given up and given out. They will give it all they've got and keep going. After all, the next time they hit that wall, it may come down!

THE LAW OF REPRODUCTION

I was walking through the streets of London when I saw a man walk out of a restaurant, and he walked just like a duck. His toes pointed out, and he took short little steps that made him appear to be waddling. His wife and kids walked out of the restaurant behind him. Those two kids looked exactly like their dad, and they walked like ducks too. That's the Law of Reproduction. A lot of the mannerisms and idiosyncrasies we have, we got from our parents, who in turn got them from their parents.

I have a fishing buddy from Texarkana, Texas, whose neck twitches. We were fishing for bass one time, and he kept twitching. Finally I said to him, "Do you need me to pray for your neck?"

He said, "I don't have anything wrong with my neck."

I said, "But you keep moving it all the time."

He said, "My father moved his neck like this."

I said, "For real?"

He said, "Yeah, my grandfather did too."

There wasn't anything wrong with his neck, but from being around his dad, he picked up the habit of twitching his neck. Because of the Law of Reproduction, you become like the people you spend time with, for good or for bad. That is why you need to choose your friends wisely. No matter what kind of family you grew up in, you can become the person you were created to be. Look around for the people you want to be like and introduce yourself. Strike up a friendship with them if possible. Go to work for them if the Lord leads you.

We all have heard the old saying, "One bad apple spoils the whole barrel," but we have to remember that the opposite is also true. If we hang around people who have a "never give up" attitude, we will begin to adopt that same character trait. If we work for and hang around those with vision and integrity, we will pursue our life's work with creativity and honesty.

WALK THE TALK

The apostle Paul had a fighting spirit and a "never give up" attitude. He was shipwrecked, stoned and left for dead, bitten by a snake, and thrown in a dark dungeon. He was whipped thirty-nine times and still didn't give up. You might ask, "How could he go through all that and still keep on? Where did he learn that kind of bulldog tenacity?"

One of the places he got it was from a man named Stephen, a mighty man of God and a follower of Jesus you can read about in Acts, chapters 6 and 7. Witnesses were bribed to lie and falsely accuse Stephen of blasphemy. A crowd gathered and became so incensed, they dragged him outside the city and stoned him. An average stoning would take anywhere from seven to nine hours because they took their time using big rocks. They would start by breaking all the toes, then the feet, then the ankles and so on. It was a slow, torturous death.

Now you remember that Paul was not always the great apostle. Before his Damascus Road experience, he was Saul of Tarsus, who terrorized Christians. It just so happened that Saul was there when Stephen was stoned. The Bible says, "Meanwhile, the witnesses laid their clothes at the feet of a young man named Saul" (Acts 7:58). He stood by and watched Stephen endure the slow, agonizing stoning.

Saul (Paul) also saw that Stephen never backed off from his testimony, nor did he get mad at God for allowing this to happen to him. In fact, in the face of a cruel and painful death, Stephen's face shown as he looked up to Heaven and asked the Father to forgive those who were stoning him. Does this sound familiar? Jesus did the same thing on the cross.

Stephen walked in faith and love even through his death. He never gave up, and he was a powerful influence on Saul. Refusing to give up in the midst of the storm, Saul saw Stephen walk his talk. If Stephen had backed down, Saul might never have become the apostle Paul. And I'm sure that when the Holy Spirit moved Paul to write verses like Philippians 4:13 NKJV, "I can do all things through Christ who strengthens me," and 1 Corinthians 13, the well-known love chapter, Paul remembered Stephen's shining face.

It's easy to be a good example when everything is going well, and you can talk all day and all night about what you believe and how people ought to live; but when the fire burns, how do you react? The way you act and the choices you make influence everyone around you, even those you least expect to influence. You may not be aware of who is watching you, and only years later hear of the impact you had on their life.

The Law of Reproduction is how the thinking, speech, and behavior of future generations are formed. Someone is always watching and waiting for you to break through the setback you are in, observing how you fight for your comeback and then go beyond it. Stephen had watched Jesus, and then Saul (Paul) watched Stephen. Later, Timothy and Titus and others would watch Paul. What will the next generation see in you? What do the people around you see in you?

It might be something as seemingly insignificant as praying over a meal at a restaurant, but when you bow your head to pray, you don't know how many others in the restaurant see you and are reminded to be thankful for what God gives to them. It may even stimulate a conversation with someone sitting nearby, someone who needs a word of encouragement at that moment in their lives. They know they can trust you because you are showing what you believe. You don't just talk about it; you live it.

If we want the next generation of believers not to cower or back down, to fight for their comebacks, to cover each other's weaknesses and lift each other up, and to stand strong in the midst of crisis, then we need to show them how it's done! We need to walk the talk. Is what we say we believe what the people in our lives see us living?

WHAT IS YOUR LEGACY?

What sort of legacy are you leaving for your children, your children's children, your relatives, the driver who cusses you out in the grocery store parking lot, the boss who blames you for his mistakes, or the co-worker who lies to get the promotion you've been waiting for? Are you demonstrating that "never give up" attitude in the face of disappointment, loss, or pain? Maybe you are going through illness, the loss of a loved one, or the pain of divorce. Whatever it is, remember the power of your influence. Someone is always watching you. If you can't do anything else, you can leave a legacy of a "never give up" attitude.

There is always hope when you know and have faith in God.

Declare out loud, "I will live a good life, regardless of setbacks! I will obtain the promises God has given me. I will live by what God says and not by what I see. I will have faith in Him, and I won't ever give up!"

It is important to hold onto those words in the midst of setbacks. Why? Because many times a setback is most difficult when you are right on the edge of your breakthrough. That's when the enemy tries to shake you and everything around you. He wants to stop you because if he can stop you, he can stop those coming after you. He wants your children to see you fail. He knows that if you make it, your success will fill them with hope and a faith-filled momentum that anything is possible.

Hang on no matter how it looks or how you feel. The Bible gives you a fantastic promise when you are fighting for your comeback: "Let us not become weary in doing good, for at the proper time we will reap a harvest if we do not give up" (Galatians 6:9). That promise is to you, your children, and your children's children.

9

YOUR FATHER

When you become a believer in Jesus Christ, you become a son or daughter of God. People say all the time, "We're all children of God," but that is really not true. Yes, God loves everyone. We know this because He sent Jesus to die for all of us. And He is doing everything He can to help each person; but only those who surrender their lives to Jesus become His actual children. The Bible says that's when He adopts us, and nothing can separate us from Him after that (Ephesians 1:5, Romans 8:39).

If you haven't ever thought about it before, you need to consider the kind of spiritual father God is. If you had a good natural father, you might relate to Him easier; but even if you had a really bad natural father or stepfather, you can get past that because God will help you to see who He really is. Then you can begin to trust Him and even love Him back.

"Why are you spending all this time talking about God being my Father? I mean, what difference does it make? I'm trying to get my comeback here!"

It is important for you to know and trust God your Father because He is the one who has planned and prepared your comeback. When you see how much He loves you and begin to trust Him for the comeback He has for you, you will accelerate your comeback. In fact, I'm going to tell you a story that illustrates this perfectly.

A BAD DECISION

A good and wealthy man had two sons. The oldest was a college football star, who graduated from college with top honors and joined the family firm. He worked hard to live up to the fine reputation established by his father and grandfather before him. The younger son was just the opposite of his brother. He just wanted to party and didn't want to work, so he asked his father for the money he would inherit upon his father's death.

Now you must understand that in this family's culture, asking for your inheritance before the death of your father was a huge insult. It showed great disrespect. Literally, it was saying, "Dad, you are dead to me now, so just give me my inheritance." That is how selfish and insensitive this son was. He dishonored his father to get what he wanted. Nevertheless, the father gave the son what he asked for and watched him drive away in his hot, red Porsche.

I want you to notice right away that even when his son dishonored him and made a terrible decision, the father still honored the son's decision. That is the way your heavenly Father is. He continues to love us and respect us even when we don't acknowledge He exists and we make very bad decisions. He will do anything to help us, but He respects our right to lock Him out of our lives.

Your Father never forces His will or His way upon you. He respects you.

DOWN THE SLIPPERY SLOPE

Life in the big city was everything the son hoped it would be— one big party after another. He rented a spacious luxury apartment in the artist district and immediately became a part of the wealthy in-crowd that stayed up all night and slept it off all day. There were lavish gatherings with all the liquor, drugs, and women he wanted. He was living in the fast lane. Nothing was outside of his grasp. He started experimenting with drugs, and before he knew it, he was hooked on crack. His habit became more and more expensive, and his inheritance was decreasing rapidly.

He needed more money, so he wrote to his father that he had a chance to do an internship with an international corporation. He convinced his father to give him his share of stock from the family firm to finance getting his future career established. His father cashed in the stock and sent him the money with his blessings.

The young man lived it up with his new "friends," supporting his own habit and often theirs as well. Within a short time he had gone through all of his money. He sold his Porsche and pawned his jewelry. His so-called 'friends' dropped out of sight when the money ran out and he lost his posh apartment. He was so strung out he couldn't hold a job even if he could get hired, and he moved into a crack house, selling drugs to get by.

By this time, the young man's body was thin and wasted. His hair and beard were long and stringy, and his clothes were dirty and ragged. Anyone who met him on the street would not have recognized him as the bright young man who had left home wearing designer clothes and driving a red sports car.

THE FACE OF AN ANGEL SPEAKS

One day the young man sold some black heroin to a beautiful teenage girl. She reminded him of a girl he had dated in high school, someone he really cared about. The next day he was wandering the streets, looking for possible buyers, when he glanced at a newsstand. There was the same girl. Her picture was on the front page of a newspaper. She was a famous lawyer's daughter and had died of an overdose. Her face, smiling like an angel, penetrated the hard shell of his heart, and he wept as he realized he had contributed to her death.

He could not take his eyes off of her. She was so alive and full of promise—but now gone forever. He realized how low he had sunk. Even in the wasted, confused state he was in, he suddenly had a clear, precise picture of himself. He saw the futility and devastation of his life. He had lost everything because of his self-centeredness and arrogance. Worse than that, he had brought death instead of life to those around him.

Still riveted to the picture on the front page of that newspaper, he knew he had to get out of the crack house and go home. He thought, *My father's employees earn a good living, and here is his son living in this pigpen of a crack house. I'll go back and ask my father to forgive me. I know I'm not worthy to be called his son, but maybe he will hire me to work for him. Even if it's just a minimum wage job and I sleep in the barn, at least I will be able to provide for my needs and live a clean life.*

In the Bible, God is good to reveal how sin works. In Hebrews 11:25 He says that sin is great for a season. Initially, sin is very pleasant. You think, *This is great! Nothing bad is happening to me. My parents and all those Christians didn't know what they were talking about.* Then slowly but surely, sin hooks you. You think either you are getting away with it or all you had heard about it being evil and destructive was a lie. But the day always comes when the enemy, who has been orchestrating the whole situation, begins to pull the rug out from underneath you. He proceeds to destroy you with the very thing that gave you pleasure in the beginning.

The son's wild self-indulgence had worked for a while, and he thought he was in full control of his life; but now he saw the truth. His pride and selfishness had put him in the hands of his worst spiritual enemies. He had hit bottom, the final setback after many setbacks, and he knew he had to change. God used the face of an angel to speak to him in his darkest, most hopeless and helpless hour. Even then, He was reaching out to him.

"I thought you said God wouldn't push Himself on anyone, that He respected the decisions of people? How did He have the right to use the picture of that girl to influence this guy?"

He was given that right by the prayers of the boy's father! All this time his father had never given up on him. He never stopped loving him, even when he received reports from good friends in the big city that his son was wasting his life and lying to him about what he was doing. He never quit believing his son would come to his senses and come home to him!

THE FIRST GOOD DECISION

This young man was smart enough to realize he was in the worst and final setback. If he didn't change direction and change his life, he would die. Somehow he had to move toward his comeback, and he knew that his comeback was the same as returning to his father. He thought, "I know I've messed up big time, and I can't go back to the position I left. I'm no longer an heir, but I'll be satisfied with just being my father's slave."

That is what the enemy always tells us in a setback, especially one we caused ourselves. He says, "You're a failure, and you'll never be what you thought you were going to be. In fact, you can't even return to where you were before you fell into this pit. It's over for you. Just get whatever job you can get, do the best you can, and at least you will have something to eat the rest of your life." In this way, the enemy may lose a little control over you, but he keeps you down.

The enemy is a liar and always has been. No matter how far you've fallen, the promises of God for your life are still in play. I know this because God says it in His Word (1 John 1:9), and I have experienced it many times! God is big enough to change the direction of your life so that you can still hit the bull's-eye He ordained you to hit. If you will take responsibility for your bad decisions, for your sins and mistakes, and then turn from them, He always forgives and cleans you up inside and outside. He always has a comeback for you!

So this wayward young man made his way back to his father. Dressed in rags, smelling like a sewer, unshaven and unclean, he turned onto the beautiful, tree-lined driveway that led to his father's house. Then something totally unexpected happened. He saw his father running toward him, as fast as a man that age could run, arms open wide, tears streaming down his face.

Before the son could take it all in, he was wrapped in his father's strong and loving arms, his warm tears bathing his face as he kissed him. Finally, his father managed to say, "I have missed you so much. I'm so glad you're back. Here, put on my coat, and let me put my ring on your finger." After doing these things, the father hugged and kissed him again and laughed, "Come! Let's go celebrate!"

The fact that the father clothed his son with his coat is highly significant. He wanted to put his son under his protection and cover him with his love and forgiveness before he presented him to anyone else. This is just like our Father! He is gracious and kind. He never berates us or shames us for what we've done, even when we have committed terrible sins against Him. He does not deny anything; He forgives everything. There is a big difference!

Stunned by his father's show of love and forgiveness, the son's feet were nailed to the ground. When he didn't move forward, his father turned and asked, "What's the matter?"

Barely able to whisper with head bowed, the boy choked on his words. "Dad, I've been so bad. You have no idea the terrible things I have done. I brought shame on you and our entire family. I threw away everything you gave me. In all this, I have dishonored you and am not worthy to be your son. You should not be around me, and I don't deserve to be treated like this. Just give me a job. I'll do anything you ask. You don't need to be nice to me."

The father's eyes grew intense. He raised his son's lowered head and made him look him in the eye. "You are my son. Nothing you do will ever make me stop loving you and wanting the very best for you. Yes, you have made some bad decisions and, no doubt, you will have some consequences to endure. Maybe we all will. But we will go through it together." He paused and put his hands on his son's shoulders.

"You have come home a different person. You left a foolish boy; you have come home a wiser, kinder man. It is my deepest desire, and it would give me the greatest pleasure to restore you and to see you flourish as my son. Please, come and celebrate this new day with me."

When the son chose to go home to be restored by his father and to reach his full potential as his son, he made the first good decision of his life. It just happened to be the best decision of his life.

HONOR FOR SHAME

The father's servants were also in shock when they saw the father and son, arms around each other, walking up to the house. When the father told them to get out the steaks to grill and make all the boy's favorite side dishes and desserts, they were probably shaking their heads saying, "Man, does he know what he's doing? Maybe he doesn't realize his son lives in the worst crack house in the city and hangs out with some really bad folk. Or maybe he's in denial. After all, he's been planning this thing for a long time."

You don't just throw together a fabulous celebration feast in an hour. When one of my staff got married, the planning absorbed a full year. I heard the bride-to-be discuss every detail. "I'm going to walk down that aisle, the train of my gown is going to be flowing, we're going to play that Bebe Winans' song, the little girls are going to throw rose petals on the aisle, and he's going to come in from the side all handsome in his tux...." On extremely important occasions, every detail is important—and it was to that father too.

That wayward son's comeback was planned way in advance.

The father had been watching and planning for his son's comeback from the moment he left. That's why he saw the son when he turned into the driveway. When he ran to him and embraced him, he didn't look at the outward appearance; he looked through the boy's eyes, saw a changed heart, and knew the time for celebration had come. His son was ready to exchange his shame for the father's honor.

If you can get this truth established in your mind and heart, you will save yourself a lot of grief and needless anxiety as you move from your setback to your comeback and beyond: The enemy gives you thoughts condemning you and shaming you for your sin, mistake, fault, or weakness; the Father gives you hope and strength to turn, learn, and overcome whatever it is that has set you back.

I'm not saying God is in denial over your problems and issues! He knows what they are and how they trap you better than you do; but His focus is on transformation, reformation, and restoration to move you forward. He never uses condemnation to motivate you out of a setback. He simply gives you the understanding of what you have thought, said, and done wrong. Then He waits for you to decide. You will either go to Him to get things straight or go out and try to fix yourself and your situation on your own. If you are smart, like the son in our story, you will run to the Father and do it His way!

THE FATHER'S COMEBACK

The story I just told is based upon the story most people refer to as "The Prodigal Son," which Jesus told in Luke 15:11-32. Jesus wants us to know that no matter how low we sink in life, the Father has a comeback prepared for us; and He'll do it again and again if we need Him to. Jesus knows the depth of the Father's love for us, and He wants us to know that love also. The truth is, we really aren't going to make it, and we aren't going to be happy or fulfill our purpose in life, without accepting the Father's love for us.

He will send people to cross our paths to bless us and reveal His love and care for us. I've had people come to me and say, "I don't know why, but I really want to give you this $10,000." I knew immediately who had given them that desire! That's my Daddy showing me how much He loves me by sending people to help me do what He's called me to do.

The Father also gently leads you to and through your comeback and beyond. Here are some steps you will have to go through to get where He wants you to go:

Step One: Get rid of your failure mentality. In the story of the prodigal son, the son went back to his father, dragging all the shame and disgrace along with him, prepared to beg for a menial job. This young man expected his father to react according to a failure mentality, keeping a record of all his wrongs. He would have counted himself lucky to get a handshake from him. He was prepared for the "look." You know what I'm talking about. You must have gotten the "look" from your parents when you were growing up. They didn't have to say a word; you just knew from their expression that you were in trouble. He was ready to hear: "You don't know what you did to your mother! We couldn't sleep for nights. You've wrecked our family's name and fine reputation. How could you do this after all we've done for you?"

The father shocked the son with a setback mentality. Failure says, "It's over. Your actions prove you are bad and will never amount to anything." Setback says, "It's not over until you quit. You can change on the inside and make a comeback on the outside." A setback is not a permanent thing. The father saw his son as a champion who had just lost a major race; he didn't see him as a loser who should never run again. That is the difference between viewing yourself as a failure instead of seeing your situation as a setback.

Like the father in the story, your Father makes a distinction between you and your actions. He will never stamp "failure" on your forehead because He sees you as a masterpiece in motion. You may have a series of bad setbacks, but if you just keep moving in His direction He will supernaturally enable you to overcome your past and succeed in life.

Even before Adam and Eve ate that forbidden fruit, our Father had a setback mentality. Their sin was devastating, but He would have the last word! Through Jesus, He extends His mercy and grace to us no matter how bad we act. He cleans us up and restores us when we turn back to Him, and then calls for a celebration. God loves to party, and His comeback parties are better than any Super Bowl party you've ever attended!

Step Two: Blast through survival mode into comeback mode. The son was in survival mode when he returned to his father's house. He was down to the bare basics: food, water, shelter, and a few clothes. He was preparing to do any kind of job to obtain the bare basics, but his father had something entirely different in mind.

Coach Vince Lombardi was like that. He took a team of losers and turned them into champions by treating them with respect. He believed that if you treat people like winners, they will act like winners. He blasted the Green Bay Packers out of survival mode into a comeback mode by training them as though they were already champions. That's what the Father does.

The moment you take responsibility for yourself and your situation and turn to God, you may have a period of time where you are concerned just about the bare basics; but that is not the full comeback God has planned for you. He wants you to move beyond that to become all He created you to be. Your Father wants you to do more than survive; He wants you to thrive. He wants to make you into the champion He created you to be.

Step Three: Write down the promises God has given to you. If you haven't written down promises that address your needs and dreams, you won't be able to remember them when you are in the battle for your comeback. Write them down and read them over and over so you will remember why God put you on this planet.

It will put that bulldog faith and never-quit fight into you when circumstances are the darkest.

Step Four: Beware of dream thieves and send them packing. The enemy is a liar and a thief, and he will send people to distract you and create circumstances to drag you down. He tries to pick your pockets and steal your dreams any way he can. He doesn't like you because you have what he has always wanted: rule on the Earth. So if he's been attacking you lately, get rid of him. You do this by simply saying, "In Jesus' name, get out!"

One of the great things about being a child of God and a member of the body of Christ is that Jesus gave us His authority over the enemy. He told us to exercise His authority by using His name. So when you sense something evil is confusing you, distracting you, annoying you, or causing you physical pain, stop and tell it to get out of your life "in Jesus' name." You are your Father's child, and the enemy has no legal rights with you. Don't let him hinder you or distract you from getting your comeback!

Step Five: Expect to obtain what God has promised you. My natural father died in a car accident when I was ten years old. My mother soon worked two shifts in a donut shop. She paid her tithes and gave offerings to several ministries, believing God would get her out of her difficult financial situation. It was tough, but no matter how bad things were, she never let her expectation level fall. She knew the Father would take care of His children.

She raised all four of us kids in the things of God and taught us how to serve Him. She stood on His promises in the Bible and walked her talk. Three of us are now in full-time ministry, slapping the enemy upside the head every chance we get. I thank God she never gave up. She didn't just survive; she overcame; and God exceeded her expectations. He likes to do that!

While you are fighting for your comeback, the circumstances may not look like what God has promised will ever come to pass. You might not feel too blessed from time to time. You may look at your bank account, and it really doesn't look blessed! But I'm telling you, believe the promises God has given you and expect them to come to pass. When God says, "I will…," you can bank on it!

LEVELS OF FAITH

To have great expectations and hope, you must have faith in the Father, who has prepared your comeback and supernaturally enables you to obtain it. You must accept His love for you because the Bible says that faith works by love (Galatians 5:6). That makes sense. If you don't believe God loves you, why would you ever believe He would do anything for you? If you believe He loves you, then you will believe He will move Heaven and Earth to get you where you need to go.

The Bible speaks of five different levels of faith: weak faith, little faith, growing faith, strong faith, and great faith.

- Abraham did *not* have *weak* faith. Even though his body was old and Sarah had been unable to bear children, he did not waver in his expectation that God would do what He promised by giving him a son (Romans 4:18-20).

- Jesus spoke to the disciples of their *little* faith, when they awakened Him in the boat to calm the raging storm (Matthew 8:26).

- Paul wrote to the Thessalonians about their *growing* faith (2 Thessalonians 1:3).

- Abraham had *strong* faith and was fully persuaded God was able to do what He promised (Romans 4:21).

- Jesus spoke of the centurion soldier's *great* faith when he asked Jesus to heal his servant (Matthew 8:5-13).

Anyone who works out knows that building muscles requires persistent stretching and pushing to higher levels. That's exactly how you build your faith. I believe I have been doing faith exercises without even knowing it. I started back in the 1980s with weak faith, then I moved to little faith. In the 1990s, I began exercising my faith muscles and my faith grew. In the mid 1990s, I was pushing for things that required strong faith. Now, in the new millennium, I realize it is going to take great faith for me to continue to move forward.

I remember when it was hard for me to believe God for a thousand dollars to go overseas. Then I had to have faith for two thousand, then ten thousand. I started exercising my faith muscles, seeing myself preaching to ten thousand, then twenty, then thirty, and on up into the hundreds of thousands. I saw myself preaching all over the world, and everything I was seeing began to happen. Now I have faith for half a million dollars when it is needed to do something for God.

What I have learned through the years is really funny. The more I see myself as God's little child, the greater my faith grows.

LIKE A CHILD

Life starts out with a shout. Think about it. You came out of your mother's womb shouting! Babies learn to cry when they are hungry or wet or hurting. Toddlers shout and laugh when they play together. Kids run up the steps, fling open the door, and shout to Mom after playing outside or when they come home from school.

We start out living life full of dreams, hopes, and expectations. We have a sense of purpose and importance. We look around and just know that we have a Father God who loves us and has a great life prepared for us. What I'm describing is childlike faith. This is the kind of faith we must have in the Father, even when we become old. Jesus said that everything about Him and His kingdom was dependant upon being like a child who loves and trusts the Father.

And he said: "I tell you the truth, unless you change and become like little children, you will never enter the kingdom of heaven. Therefore, whoever humbles himself like this child is the greatest in the kingdom of heaven."

—Matthew 18:3-4

Consider this: In a perfect world such as Heaven, the Father is a perfect father. He is the perfect combination of justice and love; accountability and mercy; responsibility and faith; knowledge and creativity; order and diversity. His holy character and His sovereign power merit your humble, childlike faith. And really, that is all He asks of you. When you humbly trust Him for everything, you literally give Him permission to do anything.

Your comeback depends upon coming home to your Father. Accept His love and forgiveness. Allow Him to restore you, celebrate you, and transform you so that you won't have to go through this setback again. And remember, no matter what happens, He is there for you!

10

SINGING IN THE DARK

"That last chapter was great if I'm in a setback I caused myself, but what about the times when I'm just minding my own business, doing the right thing, and someone blindsides me? Where's my loving heavenly Father when that happens?"

He's wherever you want Him to be.

The father in the story of the prodigal son was always there, waiting for the son to turn to him. Your heavenly Father is always there, waiting for you to come to Him in your heart. He didn't cause your setback, but He gets blamed for all kinds of things He didn't have anything to do with! Whether your best friend betrayed you or a hail storm destroyed your car, He is there to help you get through it. He's the good guy, and that is what you will see more and more as you turn to Him and spend time with Him.

Something amazing happens to you when you spend time with God. Being with Him makes you a better person. It's like being in love for the first time. Suddenly you see yourself through the eyes of Someone who respects you and adores you. You dare to believe you are the wonderful person they believe you are, and you act like it. In a human romance, this can be pure fantasy; but with God it is always the truth. He never lies, and He shows you exactly who you are and what you can become. What's more, He likes you! That's why your relationship with Him is the key to your comeback.

My father and mother had five children, and I loved it when my dad got with me one-on-one. He'd take me to Little League practice, look me in the eye, and say, "Timmy, you're going to be someone special," or, "Timmy, you're a champion." I loved those times alone with my dad because he made me feel good about myself and what I was capable of being.

Some of us get so busy making things happen, earning a degree, dating, getting married, buying a house, losing weight, playing with the dog, climbing the corporate ladder, and even serving God, that we don't take time for God. We are sliding and gliding through life, but He's trying to get some one-on-one time with us. After all, He created us to have a relationship with Him.

It's great to be reminded of what is really important in life. Sometimes we are reminded by times of sheer joy and sometimes by tragedy. It's easy to be grateful for the joyful times and love the Father for them, but in times of deep sorrow it can be difficult. We think He has forsaken us, but He is right there, waiting for us to let Him into our hurt and pain so He can comfort and heal us. He is waiting for us to let Him take us out of our setback into the comeback He's prepared for us.

Singing in the Dark

The Darkness Descends

When I was a little kid chasing the ice cream truck, flying my kite, and occasionally getting in fights with my neighbors, I never knew life could have so many strange turns. Everything was going great, and then, overnight, everything went dark. My family experienced two events that didn't just rock the boat; they were like two depth charges, and we felt like we were sinking.

My father died suddenly when I was ten, a tough age for a boy to lose his dad. Just three years later, a call came that my sister had been in a terrible car accident. We went to Modesto, California, to pray for her. She was in a coma for eight days and then died. Everybody in the family was devastated. Some began messing up big time, but I watched my mother continue to believe and trust God. She held on to Him for dear life, knowing He was her only hope.

Although her world had been plunged into darkness and she experienced two terrible setbacks right after another, my mother continued to praise God. As she praised Him and trusted Him, He filled her with a supernatural strength to raise us and to do what was needed to provide for us. His love ignited her love, which gave her the faith and courage to come back against all odds.

Later, when I was in college, some friends asked me if I wanted to go see a man by the name of Paul Yonggi Cho. We hopped into my Honda Civic and drove four hours to hear this man. He had

had tuberculosis as a teenager, was miraculously healed, and was now the pastor of the largest church in the world, which was in Seoul, Korea. In broken English he said, "You must believe the Lord." In him I saw another example of someone who praised God in the darkness and was healed. He went from setback to comeback and beyond because he believed God over everything he was experiencing.

When the darkness descends, you have a choice: You can wallow in grief and self-pity, blame God, and become self-destructive; or you can turn to God, let Him mend your broken heart, and exchange your grief for hope and your self-pity for faith. If you choose the latter, you can ask Him to show you the next step to take. Then He will supernaturally enable you to begin to move forward again.

Don't misunderstand me. When you lose someone you love, you need to go through the normal grieving process. You can't hold sorrow inside. You must release it and give it to the Lord. You must allow Him to be your Refuge. You must also allow others to comfort you and help you move through the process of grieving. Then you must move forward with God. It is unhealthy to let grief take over your life. This is allowing a setback to overtake you and rob you of the comeback God has for you.

When you decide to praise God and trust Him in your darkest hour, He will turn the lights on again. He will also give you an idea.

A GOD IDEA IS SO MUCH BETTER

There is a difference between a good idea and a God idea. Good ideas come from the mind of a human being; God ideas come from the mind of the Creator of the Universe. Good ideas might come to pass if we work on them; God ideas will certainly come to pass if we do things His way. People's good ideas are dependant upon human knowledge and strength; God's ideas are dependant upon divine revelation and power.

There is a great story about the apostle Paul and his preaching partner, Silas, in the book of Acts, chapter 16. Paul wanted to preach in Asia, but God said, "That's a good idea, but it's not My idea." As Paul and Silas continued on their missionary journey, everywhere they went God said, "No. That's a good idea, but it's not My idea."

Paul and Silas knew that if they did what they thought was a good idea, they would be proceeding in their own wisdom and power. They wanted God's supernatural wisdom and power to see them through whatever they did, so they waited for His idea. They knew He would only back His idea.

It wasn't long before Paul had a vision of a man calling them to come to Macedonia. He knew that was a God idea. Immediately he and Silas set out for Philippi, the foremost city in Macedonia. After being there for several days, Paul met a woman by the name of Lydia, a wealthy merchant in the import/export business. She was the first person to open her heart to the Good News that Jesus had come to restore us to the Father. She and her household got baptized, and she invited Paul and Silas to stay in her home. She started having meetings there and told everyone she met how Jesus had changed her life.

As Paul and Silas walked about the city, a servant girl kept harassing them in a strange way. She was crying out that Paul and Silas were servants of the Most High God, here to tell them the way to be saved. What she was saying was okay, but the way she was saying it was drawing attention to Paul and Silas, not to Jesus. Paul smelled a rat, and after three days he got God's wisdom on it: the girl was demon possessed. The enemy was using flattery to distract them!

Immediately Paul cast the demon out of the girl. All the saints were relieved and rejoiced that the girl was saved and set free. Paul and Silas were feeling good. God's idea to come to Philippi was being backed up by His supernatural wisdom and power to bring this city to Jesus. Unfortunately, the enemy didn't take this defeat lying down, and events were about to take an unexpected turn. Paul and Silas were about to have a major setback.

A ROMANS 8:28 MINDSET

The servant girl's masters were furious because Paul hit them in their pocketbook. They were using the demon-possessed girl as a fortune-teller. People paid good money to hear what the demon was telling them through the girl. When the demon was gone, she couldn't tell them anything. They dragged Paul and Silas before a judge, accused them of ruining their business, and incited the crowd against them. The judge ordered Paul and Silas to be stripped and beaten.

Now who sent Paul to Philippi? Not his mother-in-law or his financial advisor! It was God. That's right. In the middle of a God idea, all hell can still come against you because the devil hates it when you do God's will. Why? People become Christians, and his demons get kicked out of those they have enjoyed possessing. I want you to know that just because you are following God's plan and purpose, your life will not be perfect. In fact, that's when the battle gets more intense.

Before you get all freaked out, I want you to think about something for a minute. God wants to bless you and use you to do great things, but the enemy wants to destroy you and use you to destroy everyone and everything around you. There is going to be a battle until Jesus comes back and kicks the devil off the planet for good. In the meantime, you need to face facts and have faith in the God who is far greater than your enemy. Instead of getting discouraged and depressed, you need to look forward to all the miracles and signs and wonders God will do whenever the enemy tries to take you out!

This is what I call a Romans 8:28 mindset. Romans 8:28 says, "And we know that in all things God works for the good of those who love him, who have been called according to his purpose." When you act on a God idea and are committed to do things His way, when you trust Him, He will take the worst setbacks and turn them into glorious comebacks. A Romans 8:28 mindset is believing that no matter what happens, God will use it for your good—and the good of everyone around you.

That's the mindset Paul and Silas had when a whole city turned against them and things went from bad to worse. Not only were they beaten until their backs were raw, but they were chained to a wall in the deepest, darkest dungeon. Big rats probably ran around their feet, which were in stocks, stretching them to the point of almost breaking their pelvic bones.

The physical pain and torment must have been excruciating, but there was also the mental and emotional anguish of knowing what God had sent them to do and not being able to do it. It is in setbacks like these that we decide to either feel sorry for ourselves and give up or believe God meant it when He wrote Romans 8:28 to us.

SINGING HIS PRAISES

When everything that could go wrong went wrong, Paul and Silas began to pray, and that makes sense. When you are standing on the deck of the sinking Titanic, a good prayer like, "Jesus!!!" is a good response! They could have cussed God out and sent a fax to the other disciples, saying, "It's just not worth it, this business of serving God," but they prayed instead.

Paul and Silas had a Romans 8:28 mindset and believed no matter what happened to them, God would turn it to their good; so their prayer must have been something like: "Thank you, Lord, for being with us, for strengthening us, and for turning this whole situation around so that we will be free to preach the Gospel and lead more people to You."

How do I know they had this mindset and prayed this prayer? After they prayed they did something that seems totally outrageous. They began to sing praises to God! They sang praise songs through their pain, their fear, their anguish, their anger, their discouragement—and all the darkness that surrounded them in the natural realm and in the spirit realm. They were praising God in advance for answering their prayer.

Let's get real. Most of us wouldn't react that way. More than likely we would cry, "God, I must have missed You on this one. Get me outta heeere!" You can really tell what somebody is all about when they are pressed beyond the limits of their patience and endurance. What is inside of them will come out. Paul and Silas were pressed, and they sang praise to God. That says a lot about what was in them—a lot of Jesus!

I'll be honest. When I first started serving God, that's not how I responded. When I was in Bible school, I studied the Bible and prayed a lot, but I'd go through seasons of really messing up. I'd be doing really great and then just get stupid. Can you identify with what I'm saying? I'd be studying, praying, and believing God for big things; and then nobody would invite me to preach. I was called to be a preacher and no one would invite me.

I remember one night I was so mad, I decided I was going to quit the ministry. I was driving around listening to Teddy Pendergrass, "Turn Off the Lights," when I decided, "I'm not going to be a preacher. I'm going to be a Teddy Pendergrass." When little kids don't get their way, they throw a tantrum. That's what I was doing. I didn't get to preach so I was acting up. I never would have made it in the dark dungeon of Philippi!

Paul and Silas were pressed and yet they just kept praising. Can you hear the beat? They were rappin' for Jesus, "It's still gonna work. It's still gonna work." And the other prisoners heard them. Somebody is always watching your life!

"SUDDENLY" IS GOD'S STYLE

When midnight came and Paul and Silas were singing away, *suddenly* an earthquake shook the whole prison. God always shows up when you praise and worship Him, especially when you are carrying out His idea. Often, He does things suddenly. That's His style. I like what the late, great preacher E. V. Hill said about this: "I believe the angels were enjoying the song and stomping their feet to the beat, and it caused an earthquake!"

When the earthquake hit, all the doors in the prison opened and every prisoner's chains fell off. Paul and Silas had praised God, and their praises loosed everybody around them. Their singing created a supernatural atmosphere of freedom that was so powerful even the doors had to open and the chains had to come undone!

If we get loosed from chains of fear and anger and poverty and sickness, then we can loose our family and those around us. It only takes one to get out of the dungeon and help the rest. That's what Paul and Silas did. Just as suddenly as the doors opened and the chains fell off, the jailer woke up and assumed all the prisoners had fled. He drew his sword to kill himself rather than face death at the hands of his superiors for losing the prisoners. Paul knew this and immediately called out, "Don't harm yourself! We are all here!"

The jailer heard them, called for a light, and ran down to the dungeon. He fell at the feet of Paul and Silas and asked, "What must I do to be saved?"(Acts 16:30).

Paul said, "Believe in the Lord Jesus, and you will be saved—and your household"(Acts 16:31). The jailer and his entire household were saved and baptized that very night. I would call that a Romans 8:28 moment!

Suddenly there was an earthquake. Suddenly the doors flew open. Suddenly the chains fell off and the stocks came undone. Suddenly the jailor, his family, and all his servants had faith in Jesus and made Him their Refuge—just because Paul and Silas had praised God. And then, the next day, suddenly the magistrates of the town discovered Paul was a Roman citizen and knew they were in big trouble for the way they had treated him. Suddenly, he and Silas were free to go. They stopped at Lydia's house to say good-bye and encourage the saints, and then they were on to the next God idea.

A Letter of Encouragement

Scholars believe the jailor was the first pastor of the church in Philippi. No doubt he was at Lydia's house when Paul and Silas said good-bye and continued meeting with the other believers there. He was taught by Luke, the physician, and then made senior pastor of the Philippians. Later, Paul wrote a letter to the Philippians, and that letter is a tremendous encouragement to all believers—even today.

Watching a football game on television, I saw a defensive back intercept a pass and run forty yards to make a touchdown. He had a towel hanging from his pants with something written on it. One announcer said, "There's something written on his towel." Then another announcer read it to the crowd, "Philippians 4:13, I can do all things through Christ who strengthens me." The crowd went wild over the touchdown, and I went wild over what was written on that towel because I needed to hear those words that day! Those words were written to me from my Father. He used Paul, but I recognized His voice.

If Paul and Silas had given up and had run away at the first sign of trouble in Philippi, scared of that demon-possessed girl and what might happen if they cast the demon out, then there may never have been a young man making a touchdown with Philippians 4:13 written on his towel two thousand years later. He might never have made the touchdown, and he might never have been a witness to the power of praising God in all things.

Through it all, in the depths of his spirit Paul believed, God is able. He can still do it. It's going to be all right. He will take this setback and make a miraculous comeback out of it!

Let me tell you something about life: You're going to let yourself down, and people are going to put you down and let you down, but God is able to help you back up—if you keep the right attitude and believe. Have faith. Keep a Romans 8:28 attitude. You are saying, "I believe God over my circumstances. I believe God over my own stupidity. I believe God over everything I am. Even if I'm a knucklehead sometimes, God isn't a knucklehead! He can transform my thinking and enable me to rise above my mistakes and setbacks."

THE PAYOFF IN DARK TIMES

In the midst of the darkness, in the times of greatest pain, often that is when we gain our greatest revelations of God and His love for us. David wrote his greatest psalms in the midst of his deepest pain. Paul wrote most of his letters from prison.

When Paul became a Christian, the other disciples didn't want to hang out with him. They rejected him because they didn't trust him. So where did he go? He went to Arabia. That's the desert, the wilderness. When people reject you and don't understand you, you reach a point where you don't know who to call, what to do, or where to go. When you can't go forward, backward, or sideways to get out of where you are; you have to go up, and that's where you bump into God. It's in those where-can-I-go-but-God experiences that He gets you all to Himself and you hear Him most clearly.

The Bible says that Paul was in the Arabian Desert for fourteen years! What was he doing all that time? He was serving in the churches there and being taught by Jesus (Galatians 1:12, 2:1). He didn't get it secondhand from Peter or the rest of the apostles. He got it directly from the top. I believe you can live a good life based on secondhand revelation, but to live a God life you must have firsthand revelation. That's how you really get to know Him; and knowing Him reveals who you are in a way that sticks with you forever.

Carl Lewis had a revelation that he was a great runner. He knew he was created to run fast and to win. He was so confident that people thought he was cocky, but he worked hard and trained hard. He was so set on winning, he didn't even look for anybody else in the race and was famous for the way he threw out his chest, flew across the finish line, and went looking for the gold medal.

When you have a revelation right from God that you are a winner who is destined to accomplish certain things, the dark times of pain and suffering, of waiting and watching, of training and learning—are times when you can praise Him and enjoy His presence in your life. Furthermore, when you get out of that dark time and the enemy is there to try and stop you from doing what you know you were born to do, you are not going to back down, give up, or sing the blues. You are going to continue to sing praises to the God of your comeback!

I remember the pain and loneliness I felt when my dad died and again when my sister died, but I took refuge in the Refuge. I discovered that when I forced myself to praise and worship Him, He comforted me. He strengthened me. And He gave me ideas. He told me the next step to take. Yes, there were times when I ran from Him and messed up what He wanted to do in my life, but I have always returned to Him for my comeback. Today, I don't ever want to leave Him again. I want to live my life with Him, praising Him for all He has done, all He is doing, and all He is going to do.

I have learned that when the last thing I want to do is praise God, that's when I need to praise Him. You see, something happens when you praise God. He comes on the scene and invades your space with His peace and power. It is spiritual, but it is tangible. David knew this when he wrote Psalm 22:3. He said God literally inhabited his praises—and He's still doing it today!

When you hit a setback and things get really dark, praise the only One who can give you peace and show you the way out.

Let the righteous rejoice in the LORD and take refuge in him; let all the upright in heart praise him!

—Psalm 64:10

11

BECOMING GOD'S CHAMPION

"You said that I should be realistic. Well, I am being realistic, and it doesn't look good. There are so many problems! I'm wondering if everything I'm doing is worth it. I mean, being *realistic*, it looks like there is no way I can do this."

There are two types of realists: unbelieving realists and believing realists. Unbelieving realists look at the facts and the information available to them and make decisions based on what they know by natural means. They make choices based upon human thought and natural data. Believing realists are called believers because they believe what God promised them over anything they encounter in the natural realm of life. They don't *deny* the circumstances; they believe God can *change* the circumstances, *use* the circumstances to their advantage, or *overcome* the circumstances altogether. They make decisions based upon what God has said to them deep in their hearts, which is divine revelation.

When divine revelation, or a God idea, overrides your human thinking and knowledge, your faith in God releases Him to perform miracles in your life, miracles of all shapes and sizes. I'm all for education and training in the fields you are called to master, but you had better have a divine revelation, an understanding from God that this is His will and way for you. The reason is because when all hell breaks loose, you have to know deep in your heart that He sent you into that mess! If He sent you in, He will get you out. Remember, He has already prepared a comeback for whatever setback you encounter.

GIANTS, GRASSHOPPERS, AND GOD

When God used Moses to lead the people of Israel out of Egypt, He promised them a new land. It was a God idea. In fact, the Promised Land was the land He had given to their ancestor Abraham. He gave it to him and to all his descendants. After the miraculous trek through the parted Red Sea, God brought them straight to the border of the Promised Land and said, "This is it! Check it out." (See Numbers 13.)

It was never a question of whether or not the people of Isreal could possess the land; it was just a matter of surveying what was there and what they needed to do to possess it. Like a proud dad who has spent all night putting together his kid's first bicycle, God wanted them to see how bountiful and beautiful their land was. He wanted them to see everything He had prepared for them.

Moses chose twelve men to explore the land. He said, "Walk through the land and see what it is like. Is the soil fertile or does it need work? Bring back whatever fruits and vegetables are there. And find out what kind of people live there and how many there are. Do they live in fortified and armed cities? We want to know exactly what we are up against, if anything."

Moses was a believing realist. He acted upon God's idea to check out the land, believing God would deliver what He had promised. The twelve men did what Moses told them to do and returned carrying huge baskets of fruit. They confirmed that what God had promised was true. The land was beautiful and rich with food. They also reported that the cities were very large and heavily fortified, and the people living in the land were powerful. Among them were the descendants of Anak, old enemies of Israel who were giants.

Now we are going to see who are the unbelieving realists and who are the believing realists. Without even thinking, Caleb (one of the twelve spies) spoke his heart: "We should go up and take possession of the land, for we can certainly do it"(Numbers 13:30). Both Caleb and Joshua believed what God had promised: the land was theirs. If the land was theirs, and God had given it to them, He would see that they possessed it—giants and all.

Then the other ten spies argued, ""We can't attack those people; they are stronger than we are...We seemed like grasshoppers in our own eyes, and we looked the same to them" (Numbers 13:31,33). They went so far as to say that not only did they feel like grasshoppers, but they were sure the giants saw them as grasshoppers. How did they know this? They believed what they saw and discounted what God had said.

When the spies gave their reports, Caleb and Joshua were the only believing realists. They didn't deny there were challenges ahead, but they also knew God was bigger and His promise and power were greater than anything they faced. After all, He had just parted the Red Sea for them! Unfortunately, the people went with the ten unbelieving realists. Basically, they freaked out over the giants and adopted the grasshopper mentality. As a result, God postponed Israel taking the land for forty years, until that generation died. None of those who adopted the grasshopper mentality entered the Promised Land!

What is really interesting about this is that forty years later, when Israel went in to take the Promised Land, one of the inhabitants told Joshua, "We were scared stiff of you guys! We had heard how your God had freed you from Pharaoh, parted the Red Sea, and done all these miracles to get you here. We figured it was only a matter of time before you took over. I decided a long time ago that I wanted to be on the side of you and your God!" (See Joshua 2:9-13.)

The lesson learned here is that when God gives you a promise, don't back off of it, regardless of the circumstances. When you are facing giants and all you have is a promise from God, remember that the grasshopper mentality will abort God's comeback. You must slay any sign of a grasshopper mentality if you want to move out of your setback into your comeback.

SLAY THE GRASSHOPPER MENTALITY

The ten Israelite spies saw nothing but defeat because they had a grasshopper mentality. They saw themselves as grasshoppers and believed (mistakenly) that the giants and all the people in the Promised Land did too. It was true, the giants had a nasty reputation and the cities were great and fortified; but Israel and her God also had a reputation that preceded them, and even the giants were terrified of them!

Caleb and Joshua didn't know that the inhabitants of the Promised Land were afraid of the people of Israel, but they knew what no one else knew: They didn't look like grasshoppers in God's eyes, and His were the only eyes that counted. They knew this because they believed His promise over what they faced. The grasshopper mentality believes God is small and weak and unable to help. They grasshopper mentality can also believe God is able but not willing to help. They says things like, "Why would God be bothered with the problems of little, 'ole me? He's got the universe to run." Precisely! Helping His people is running the universe!

The ten looked like grasshoppers *in their own eyes*. It was their own perception, and human perception can be deceiving. Unfortunately, it is a law that you will get what you believe, say, and act upon. Remember the old saying, "What you see is what you get"? It's an old saying because it is a biblical principle that always holds true. If you see yourself as a loser and say you are a loser, that's what you will be. Again, the grasshopper mentality will kill your dreams and the destiny God has for you.

Do you remember the cowardly lion in the movie, *The Wizard of Oz?* Everyone knew he was a lion, but he didn't have a clue he was a *lion.* He was afraid because he didn't know who he really was. Don't be like the cowardly lion. God sees you as a champion because he made you to be a champion. That is the reality. Your enemy knows you are a champion, so he does everything he can to convince you that you aren't!

Until you slay the grasshopper mentality and believe God's promise is greater than your circumstances, until you see yourself as His champion and begin to speak and act like the champion He made you to be, you will allow the giants to steal everything He has for you, including your comeback.

Dealing With Giants

Over the years I have identified three major giants that we face in a setback. They encourage you to have a grasshopper mentality. These big guys sit on every promise, vision, and dream God has given you and dare you to knock them off. Unfortunately, many people never do knock them off, or they never knock off all of them. They just deal with one or two and let the other one(s) steal their life from them. These three giants have been stealing promises from God's people for thousands of years, and they are just as powerful today as they were in the days of Moses.

Giant #1—Fear

The first giant is fear. Fear almost defeated the cowardly lion. Fear did defeat the people of Israel who believed the ten spies instead of Joshua and Caleb. Fear is an emotion of alarm and agitation caused by the expectation or realization of danger. Have you ever heard fear defined as <u>F</u>alse <u>E</u>vidence <u>A</u>ppearing <u>R</u>eal? If God calls you to do something great, a giant fear always attacks you.

This giant will sit on your shoulder and whisper all kinds of "What ifs" in your ear. It will put pictures of calamity, tragedy, and failure in your head. Fear is one of the enemy's best tools, and there is only one way to defeat it: Throw out the negative and scary what ifs, thoughts, and pictures and replace them with what God has said to you. It might be a verse of Scripture that you read and it just leaped into your heart or something the Spirit of God told you years ago and you know it is true.

Hold onto the truth! Keep your focus and faith on God. Allow His peace and sovereign power to drive out all fear.

Giant #2—Doubt

The second giant is doubt. Doubt means to be undecided or skeptical about something. It's a lack of conviction. It's being double-minded. One minute you're up, the next minute you're down. You say, "Well, I'm pretty sure it will work, but I'm not too sure." Doubt is a crack in your faith. You haven't really decided you trust God 100 percent. You still think He may not come through for you.

There is only one way to deal with doubt. You stop it at the thought level. The moment you have a picture in your mind or an idea floats through that is contrary to what God has promised you, you throw it out! Then you fill your mind with pictures and ideas that illustrate what He has promised and will do. You turn your focus upon what He has given you to do right now and do it.

If you don't catch doubt in your mind, you will hear it coming out of your mouth! Then you need to say, "Oh God, forgive me," and declare the truth, which is what He has said to you. When you think and speak words of faith, you will close up any gaps of doubt that have crept in.

Giant #3—Unbelief

The third giant is unbelief, which obviously means not to believe. With doubt, you believe but have a hole in that belief. With unbelief, you simply do not believe. To believe means to place complete trust in or confidence in someone or something, so when you have unbelief, you are saying, "I just don't believe God will do what He said He would do."

Let me ask you this. If you don't believe God will do what he says He will do, who do you believe? There are only three choices left: yourself, another human being, or the enemy. Think about it. You know the enemy is a liar and only wants to hurt you. You know you are not 100 percent trustworthy; in fact, no human being is 100 percent faithful to everything they say. Who do you know who is? God is the only one.

To get rid of unbelief, you have to build your faith in God; and lucky for you, He told you in His Word how to do that! Romans 10:17 says that faith takes hold of your life and banishes all unbelief by "hearing" the Word of God. "Hearing" means to hear in your heart. Your ears don't just physically hear and your eyes don't just physically see the words, but the words go deep into your heart and become a part of you. God's words are seeds that can only produce faith in Him that He will do what He promised to do.

Did you know that words are seeds planted in your mind and heart? Seeds will always produce after their own kind, just like in the natural world. If you plant a corn seed, you are going to get a harvest of corn, not potatoes. In the same way, if you hear your friends say you will never amount to anything, those seeds will produce insecurity and self-hatred. That's why you have to be careful what you hear and see. Do the words you hear and see produce faith or fear, hope or discouragement, love or hate, and so on?

The words God wrote to you in the Bible are supernaturally charged to produce faith in Him and His promises to you. His words carry divine DNA and miraculously transform your mind to think like Him and act like Him. Unbelief in your heart simply melts away in the face of the supernatural power behind God's Word. There's a verse that really says it all. Hebrews 4:12 NLT says, "The word of God is alive and powerful."

To defeat all of the giants—fear, doubt, and unbelief—just get in the Bible. Find a translation that is easy for you to read and understand. Read it. Study it. Meditate on it during your day. Instead of worrying about the stock market or your kid's grades or whether or not you're going to be laid off, think about the verses you read that morning. Measure all things in your life by it. Let it be your standard and your guide in your walk of faith. Then you will be a believing realist and slay the grasshopper mentality and its giants.

If you look to other people, even other Christians, for your standard of faith, you will fluctuate from day to day; but if you measure yourself by God's Word, you will build your faith in Him more and more each day. You will see that your giants of fear, doubt, and unbelief are small and impotent when they are put up against Him and His love for you.

Do you remember the first U.S. Olympic basketball Dream Team? It was comprised of NBA greats Michael Jordan, Magic Johnson, Larry Bird, Charles Barkley, David Robinson, Patrick Ewing, Scottie Pippen, Clyde Drexler, Karl Malone, John Stockton, Chris Mullin, and Christian Laettner—probably one of the most prestigious lists in basketball history. They went into the Olympics knowing they had the best team in the world. They could whip everybody, and they did! There was no fear, no doubt, and no unbelief in those boys. They didn't look at the other teams and feel like grasshoppers; they knew who they were and what they could do.

You are part of God's Dream Team! Now I'm not talking about being arrogant, obnoxious, and self-centered; I'm talking about having a realistic understanding that you are His child, He loves you, and He will move Heaven and Earth to see that you are protected and have everything you need to succeed. I'm talking about knowing who you are and what you can do through Jesus Christ who strengthens you. That was what was written on the towel of that football player, and it was the truth!

WHY YOU NEED TRUTH

If you don't have God's truth on a matter or an issue, then you won't be able to overcome your setbacks and get to His comeback. I'll tell you why. Only His truth is going to hold you steady and keep you strong when you encounter the giants and are tempted to see yourself as a grasshopper.

Every time you have a God idea, someone or something will challenge your mission to carry it out. You can't avoid this, but God will always be your strength to overcome it. Expect the opposition and prepare yourself for it. Many people who have a God idea never get through the opposition, and they never fulfill their purpose or destiny because they thought it would just be a walk in the park. They didn't know they were going to have to fight their way out of setbacks to come back and go beyond.

When you act on a God idea, accept that you are going to have to face and do battle with some old enemies and some new enemies. Most of the Israelites thought that once they were out of Pharaoh's territory and into the Promised Land, everything would be perfect. They thought they would just march in and have a great life. Let me tell you something. God gives you the sight, the right, and the might to do great things, but you have to develop the fight!

The only way you are going to be able to fight your way through and take your promised land is by knowing the truth and not budging from it. It's not enough just to know what God said; you must believe it, live it, and refuse to back off of it. The twelve men that went in to spy out the Promised Land were the best Israel had to offer. All of them knew the promise God had made to them, but only two, Joshua and Caleb, stuck with it. They chose God's truth over human opinion and natural circumstances. That's the fight you have to win in order to get your comeback.

Be careful with whom you choose to associate. Don't spend time with negative people. It rubs off. Their words will kill your faith. If God gives you the idea of selling real estate, they will say, "You can't sell houses in this area. This is a very depressed community." If God gives you the desire to move to Los Angeles, they will say, "There is a huge fault running through there and one day the whole state of California is going to collapse into the ocean." Doesn't that sound just like the ten unbelieving spies?

Isn't it amazing that when you face opposition to a God idea, the enemy says, "This is the worst problem you have ever faced. You can't do this." Don't buy into his lie! No matter how impossible the circumstances appear to be, God has prepared a way. He will not tell you to accomplish something without giving you the means to do it.

CONTEND FOR THE PROMISE

I want to give you a three-way remedy to kick giants off your promise.

1. You must have proper knowledge.

2. You must have proper relationship.

3. You must have proper experience.

Knowledge brings things into the right perspective. When you are fighting a giant you have to be knowledgeable about the situation in order to bring it into perspective and eliminate the fear, doubt, and unbelief. In the military it is said you must know the enemy in order to prepare a winning battle strategy. This is true in spiritual battles as well. The Bible says in Hosea 4:6 that God's people are destroyed for lack of knowledge.

Some of the things we fear really aren't that scary after we get the right knowledge, relationship, and experience. I found that out when a minister friend of mine asked me to go with him for a week to Calgary in Alberta, Canada, to spend some time praying and seeking the Lord. I said, "Okay, that sounds great."

Then he said, "I'm going to take my bow and arrow, and I want to buy you one."

I said, "I'm not really into bows and arrows. I'm from the city."

He said, "Come on, it's fun, great recreation." So he bought me a bow and some arrows and paid for lessons on how to shoot at a target.

I said, "Fine, I'll go shoot at a target."

This guy was a bit of a comedian and two days before the trip he said, "Now listen. We're going bear hunting with bows and arrows."

I said, "Well, forget you! I'm not going bear hunting with any bow and arrow. I'm afraid of bears! I don't even like to go to the zoo."

He said, "It's too late. The trip is already paid for. Tim, you need some adventure in your life. You're always caught up in helping everybody else, this is going to be good for you."

What could I do? I said, "Okay, I'll go and shoot targets. Maybe one time I'll go out there with you, but hunting bears is not for me. I want to go fishing or something else."

We arrived in Canada and I discovered he had found out my size and bought me a complete camouflage outfit. Then he told me I had to paint my face. Can you picture that? Then the guides knew I was no great hunter. They laughed and teased me about how afraid I was of bears. All night around the campfire, they told stories about bear attacks. They said bears can run faster than horses and climb trees. It was bear night.

I was so freaked out I couldn't sleep. Every time I heard the tent move, I would start praying, "Oh Jesus." The next morning we were up at the crack of dawn, which was fine with me since I hadn't slept a wink anyway. We were each assigned a hunting guide. Mine was the youngest in the group, twenty-two-years-old, chewing tobacco and spitting. I was not excited about this excursion! I decided money talks so I said to my guide, "I'll pay you extra money. This is just between you and me. Don't take me around any bears. Do you understand? I don't want to see any bears."

He said, "Okay. I'll take you to an area where we haven't seen any bears for weeks. Just do what I say 'cause they're already teasing you."

If you've never been on a bear hunt let me enlighten you as to how this works. They take you out in the woods, and you have to climb up on this thing called a tree stand. Then they put out bait about twenty yards away and cover it with branches. They throw out some donuts with syrup to try to lure the bear.

My trusted guide took me to my tree stand and said, "Don't worry about anything. You ain't gonna see no bear."

I was feeling good as I climbed up on the tree stand. I had on my boots, my camouflage suit, and my green hat. My face was painted up real good. Then my guide told me to rub this scent on so the bear couldn't smell me. It was made with fox urine and came in a tube. That is where I drew the line. This city slicker wasn't about to put that on!

I was all settled down in the tree, and all of a sudden I heard, "Blaaaa, Koahhhh!" There was Gentle Ben in the flesh. This bear was tearing through the woods crushing everything in his path. I've never been so scared in my life. I had only been shooting a bow and arrow for two days. I don't like heights. I don't like the wilderness. I don't like bears. I was shaking so hard my teeth were chattering. I was thinking about what those guys said, "They'll climb trees, rip your face off, and chase you down if you try to run." My life was passing before my eyes. I was finished for sure.

The bear came closer. He was sniffing the air. I thought, *Why didn't I put on that fox urine?* He was sniffing the air and I knew he smelled me. He saw me, even though I tried to hide behind a little branch of the tree. I prayed like I had never prayed before.

When he stood up on his hind paws, I got so scared I honestly thought, *I'm going to jump out of this tree and just let him kill me quickly.* I was staring down the throat of a big bear with only a bow and arrow. No gun, no knife. Honestly, it was torment.

This bear was smart. That's how he got so big because no one had gotten him yet. He looked for the donuts, making sure his body was shielded from where I was. He was watching me the whole time. He got himself a glazed donut, staring at me as he licked his chops. He gobbled down his donut and took off crashing through the woods down toward the river.

I breathed a sigh of relief, "Thank you, God." Then back he came for more food. This time he was really growling and snarling—not a good sign. He was mad. He was agitated. And then my training in the truth kicked in. The good seed I had planted all those years came up fast!

I was experiencing the worst fear I had ever known, but suddenly the knowledge I had learned surfaced in my mind. The man who had given me the bow and arrow lessons had said, "You're such a bad shot, I'm going to give you this video on where to shoot a bear, and how to know what is happening in the mind of a bear." I watched that video over and over again. Now that valuable knowledge was going to keep me from perishing!

I got mad because I was shaking like a leaf. I remembered what the man said in the video. He said, "When you hunt a bear, don't hit it in the foot, you'll just aggravate him. Don't hit it in the head or the buttocks, or you'll just make him mad. Try your best to maneuver yourself to get a good shot at the vitals. Hit it right in the chest."

This bear had been working me over for almost a half hour. I couldn't take it any longer. He gave a great growl and made the mistake of stretching up too far. I knew it was now or never and shot an arrow toward his chest. It missed, but the bear figured out someone was shooting at him and ran off into the woods.

I don't believe in killing animals for sport, and I will never go bear hunting again, but I do believe in staying alive if a dangerous animal attacks! When the guide found me, I wish I could have jumped down and strutted my stuff, but I was still shaking because I thought the bear would bring his family back. Being from the streets of LA, I knew the big bear gang was coming back to help their cousin finish me off!

Courage Under Fire

The knowledge I gained from the video, the relationships I had with my instructor and my guide, and past experiences of God delivering me from danger—these are the things that saved my life that day in the woods.

A lot of people believe that if they are afraid, then fear has overcome them and they are cowards. That is just what the devil wants them to believe! The truth is, it was normal for me to be afraid of that bear, but ultimately I didn't allow my fear, any doubts, or unbelief to rule my thoughts or actions. I prayed, I took appropriate action, and I was okay in the end. Think about this. Courage doesn't happen without fear, doubt, and unbelief; courage overcomes all of these things to get the job done.

How do we knock off fear or doubt or unbelief? Simple faith in God. At that moment in the tree stand, my faith in God was the bottom line. I realized He had seen to it that I had the proper knowledge, He had put me in proper relationships, and I remembered all the times He had kept me alive in the past. He didn't put me in the woods to leave me and let a bear get me, and He won't drop you in the water to let you drown. He won't lift you up to let you down. When you truly know Him, you can trust Him—even when your body is shaking so bad your teeth feel like they are going to fall out!

I remembered that before David faced Goliath, he had killed a lion and a bear with his bare hands to protect the sheep he was watching. You can read about this in 1 Samuel 17:31-37. That's why he showed no fear of the giant. He knew that if God had given him victory over a lion and a bear, He would certainly give him victory over a giant that was trying to destroy His people.

I was with a pastor who was building a large 4,500-seat church. They were halfway into the building project but the money wasn't coming in. He said to me, "Every time I drive by that church, it's like the building yells, 'I will never be built!' I finally realized it was the voice of the enemy."

Your giants will shout at you too. "You'll never lose weight! God is going to make you stay single and alone the rest of your life! You don't have the faith to be healed! Your kids are going to stay messed up! Yeah, God helped others out of their setbacks, but you are too far gone!"

God is bigger than any giant or setback, and if you just have the courage to stick with Him, He'll get you through it. When the giants are screaming your worst fears, just keep shouting back, "God is greater! He will see me through this! I can do all things through Jesus who strengthens me, and that includes getting out of this mess!"

Stay close to God, the Father who loves you and will see you through any problem. By calling on Him and immersing yourself in His Word, which is the truth, you will slay the grasshopper mentality and the giants of fear, doubt, and unbelief. You will be like Joshua and Caleb, marching into your promised land as God's champion.

12

DESPERATE FAITH

When I was up in that tree stand, facing a huge bear that wanted to have me for dinner, I got desperate! There was only one name that was coming out of my mouth, and that was "Jesus!" Desperate circumstances trigger desperate faith. When you run out of rope, you will grab onto whatever faith you have. You come to the very end of yourself and your human abilities and resources—and that is a good thing.

"What! You have the audacity to tell me, when I'm too tired to even tread water anymore, I'm drowning and gasping for breath, that that's a good thing? I don't think so!"

Hear me out. Sometimes you have to get to the end of yourself and give up trying to fix your life before God can fix you. As long as you are flailing around in the water, trying to save yourself from drowning, He can't go near you; but once you let go and surrender to Him, He can reach down and pull you out.

When I was a little kid, I struggled in school. My teacher said I was the biggest clown she had ever had in class, and my reading skills were especially bad. I had ADHD and mass creativity mixed with Slurpies and red licorice. Losing my dad made things worse, but my mother kept telling me, "You can make it!"

I know my mother was desperate. Her son was an accident happening all over the place, and she needed help. Her desperate faith cried out to God for help, and He answered her prayers. About the time my dad died, I had a Little League coach named Ron Trejo. I needed a man in my life to believe in me, and Coach Trejo told me, "Tim, you've got championship qualities, but you have a bad attitude and a bad temper. You've got to stop cussing everybody out if you're going to be the person I know you can be."

I had a simmering rage inside me, but I was encouraged by what my coach was telling me. He continued to believe in me and remained in my life even after I left his team. Into my teenage years, Coach Trejo kept coming by the house to make sure I was okay. He touched my life in a powerful way, taught me discipline, and helped change me from a frightened, angry boy to a more confident, compassionate young man.

Fifteen years later, I was able to return the great gift of encouragement he had given me. I looked out my window and saw him walking across the street toward my office. He told me he was facing a desperate situation. It was my turn to say to him, "You can make it! Don't take a step back. You can get up from that situation and go forward. Get up one more time. Come on, it's inside of you." He didn't step back; he came back and coached more teams to win numerous titles.

FAITH GRASPS MIRACLES

What is a miracle? It's something we cannot explain in natural terms. It's something we know no human being did or could do. It's beyond our abilities or it overrides the laws of nature. So the only way we are going to have a miracle is if what we need is beyond our ability or the natural course of things. That's a scary place to be, and it makes us desperate. Isn't it interesting that God is often the last resort when things get bad?

We can learn a great deal from a woman in the Bible who demonstrated desperate faith in the book of Mark, chapter 5. She had been bleeding for more than twelve years and had exhausted both her strength and finances seeking help from the medical community. No one could help her. She was considered unclean and untouchable according to the laws of her culture.

She was sick and tired of being sick and tired when she heard about Jesus. Some people said He was the Son of God. She heard He would touch people and they would get well. She heard He had even raised someone from the dead. Surely, if she could just touch His clothes, she would be healed. He was her last hope. She would touch Him and be healed—or die trying, because the laws of her people said she was unclean and couldn't touch anyone. She might be stoned if they caught her touching anyone.

When she found Jesus, the crowd surrounding Him was overwhelming. It looked as though she would never be able to move close enough to touch Him, but she didn't let that stop her.

She did what she had to do. She dropped to her hands and knees and started crawling through the dust, dirt, and donkey dung. All she could see were sandals and dirty feet, but she didn't give up. She kept saying, "I will live life again. I will be a wife to my husband again. I will be healed." Imagine how she felt when she saw the hem of Jesus' robe. There He was, right in front of her, and so she reached out and grabbed hold of His clothes.

The Bible says the crowed was pressing Jesus on every side as He made his way along the street. That made it very slow going! There was hardly room to breathe. Suddenly He stopped and said, "Who touched me?"

Jesus' disciples thought He had lost it because there were so many people around Him. They said, "Everyone is touching you!"

He said, "It's a different kind of touch. I felt healing power go out of Me."

The woman hadn't even touched Jesus' skin, but He had felt her touch. It was the supernatural touch of desperate faith. She stood, completely whole for the first time in twelve years, and admitted she was the one. He said, "Woman, your faith has made you whole."

This woman did four important things:

1. She heard about Jesus.

2. She believed Jesus was the Son of God who could do miracles.

3. She said in her heart, "If I can just get to Him, I will be healed."

4. She put action to what she believed, feet to her faith, and
fought for her comeback.

HE'S STILL DOING MIRACLES

Today we are so sophisticated and well-educated that too many
people—even most Christians—don't believe God does miracles
anymore. Some people don't even believe in God. That is really
sad! But I believe God knows that and is just waiting for us to get
in a desperate situation, where only His supernatural intervention
will make things right. Then He can prove again that He not only
exists but He cares deeply about every aspect of our lives.

This was brought home to me a few years back when I met a
little seven-year-old boy. He had reached a point of desperation
and heard about me. Like the woman who was bleeding heard of
Jesus and decided to get to Him, this little boy decided he was
going to get to Tim Storey. I had just finished speaking at a church
and was in a back room when they brought him to me. I found
out later he had had to fight to get there.

He had told the ushers, "I must talk to Tim Storey right now."

They said, "He's too tired. He's been praying for people all
night. You should have come up during the prayer time."

He insisted, "No, I must talk to Tim Storey *alone!*"

One of the ushers came into the room and told me there was a
little boy who wanted to see me. I said it was okay, and in came this
little guy. He said, "Hey, heart-to-heart talk between me and you."

I said, "Okay," and asked everyone to give us some space.

He said, "You're gonna heal me, 'cause I got a problem."

I said, "Okay."

He leaned real close and whispered, "Just between me and you, I wet the bed."

I said, "You know everybody's done it."

He said, "But it messes me up, man. I can't go to Boy Scouts or to Little League sleepovers. So, go ahead and heal me." I prayed for him and sent him on his way.

Sometime later, I was preaching at another church in the same city. Walking through the crowd, I felt somebody yanking on my jacket. I looked around and saw a little boy standing there. He said, "Hey, I'm the guy you prayed for," and named his church. I see so many people, I didn't remember him. He said, "Remember what my problem was?"

I said, "Help me out."

With a slam dunk motion he smiled broadly and yelled, "No more wet sheets!"

Jesus said we could learn a lot from children, and we can learn a lot from this little boy. He heard about a man who prayed for people and they got well. He believed what he heard, and then he acted upon what he believed. Fortunately, he believed and acted upon what was true. When I pray in the name of Jesus and release my faith, He heals them. He's still doing it today just like He did it when He walked the Earth with us.

There are other things kids are hearing today that are not the truth, and that is causing them to get into a lot of trouble. I believe it is time for us as Christians to get some desperate faith that will lead to miracles that will reveal that Jesus is still the way, the truth, and the life. There are a lot of counterfeit spiritual leaders out there, saying, "Follow me! I can turn your desperate situation around!" They don't lead people to eternal freedom and peace; what they offer may look okay at first, but ultimately they lead them in the opposite direction.

I thank God that little boy heard about me, someone who follows Jesus, so that I could show him the way to life not death in his desperate situation.

WHO LEADS YOU?

My favorite miracle story of all time is about a childhood friend named Mikey. Every neighborhood has a Mikey. He was nine and I was eight. He came to me and said, "Timmy, we're gonna play hide-and-seek in the sewers underneath the rich neighborhoods."

I said, "That doesn't sound too cool."

He said, "No, it's great fun. We get flashlights and it's real dark, just right for hide and seek."

I said, "You all go ahead." You see, I was a clean freak, and tramping through a stinky, dirty sewer was not my idea of a fun time.

They took off and came back all muddy, smelling horrible, but they had had the time of their lives. The next time, I agreed to go along with Mikey and about seven other guys our age.

When you're that age, you don't read the LA Times or watch the weather channel to see what the weather will be that day. Besides that, when you are down in the sewer, you don't know when it starts to rain. So we were down in the sewer having a blast playing hide-and-seek when it began to rain. In California it doesn't just rain, it pours. Suddenly, we noticed that the water level was rising where we were hiding.

In case you have never had the pleasure of being in a sewer, let me explain. There are different size drums, but the best hiding places were in the smaller ones. We had little guys hiding in these smaller drums when the water started to rise. We thought we were going to drown for sure because the drums would fill up completely.

We started running toward the larger drums, screaming and crying, dropping our big flashlights along the way. It was complete chaos, and I realized we were totally lost. I was experiencing some desperate faith! Then I realized that we needed Mikey. I said, "Wait a minute. Where's Mikey? We gotta find Mikey."

Mikey loved those sewers and knew them like the back of his hand. He was the Sewer King. Just then, he appeared. I yelled, "Okay Mikey, lead us out of here!" Quickly I lined up all the kids, one behind the other. Each one held onto the belt of the one in front of him, and Mikey was in front of all of us.

Mikey started running with everything he had through the rising water. We were holding on for dear life to the kid in front of us. We went left. The water was coming up fast there too. Then we went right. Although it was still scary, we knew Mikey knew exactly where he was going.

Not one kid stopped and asked, "Are you sure you know which way you're going?" When you are desperate, you look for the person who knows the way out. We needed someone to lead us out of the storm sewers. We needed someone who had answers. So, Mikey led us through the maze of the sewer system.

An important detail to know in exploring the sewer system is which manhole you should pop open to get out. If you come out of the wrong one, you will get your head cut off. Mikey knew the right manhole to go to. The water was coming up higher and higher when he stopped, climbed up a ladder, and popped off a manhole cover. One by one we scrambled up after him and came out to the street. We collapsed on the pavement, trying to catch our breath. All of us were safe because Mikey was the Sewer King. In that place of desperation, we looked for someone who knew the way.

It's interesting that when Jesus announced who He was, He said, "I am the way." He knows the way out of any sewer you are in. Whether you climbed into it through your own bad decisions, fell into it by accident, or someone pushed you in—He cares about you and wants to lead you out. In fact, He does some of his greatest miracles leading us out of filthy, stinking sewers!

When you are in a desperate situation, desperate faith has a way of blowing the ceiling off your expectations. Suddenly nothing is impossible for God, and you remember that He is in the miracle-working business. You think to yourself: *If He could make Heaven and Earth, He can find me a job. If He could part the Red Sea and bring the children of Israel to the Promised Land, He can bring me to the person I will spend the rest of my life with. If He has numbered every hair on my head, He knows what's wrong with my body and how to fix it. He can do anything! I think I'll let Him lead me.*

It Had to Be God!

Lee Iacocca, former president and CEO of Chrysler, invited me to his home for dinner one evening. After dinner we sat in the living room and he said, "Mr. Storey, tell me the secret of your success."

A little nervous about how to respond, the only reply that was completely truthful was, "It had to be God."

That dinner and conversation was a God idea that opened the door for us to become friends. This was a miracle to me. I had a desperate faith to meet people who had changed the world, who were history makers, and God moved to fulfill that dream.

You can live an "it had to be God" life as well. One day your family could be restored and healthy relationships established.

People who knew you in the past would ask how you did it. The only thing you can say about a miracle like that is, "It had to be God." You could get a job, get one promotion after another, and eventually move out of gang territory into a nice neighborhood. Whenever anyone is amazed at your testimony, you only can say, "It had to be God."

The places God can take you and the people He can connect you to are unlimited when you operate in a desperate faith that knows no limitations. Desperate faith makes you totally open to God ideas, no matter how ridiculous they may seem, and God ideas always involve His supernatural working. There is no ceiling to what He can do.

In Mark, chapter 2, there is a story that dramatically illustrates what God does with the "ceilings of limitation" we place on our lives. Four friends of a paralyzed man wanted to bring their friend to Jesus so he could be healed, but the house where Jesus was speaking was packed. They couldn't get in, but they had a God idea.

They carried their friend on a stretcher up to the roof of the house and proceeded to cut a hole in the ceiling. They tied ropes to the four corners of the stretcher and lowered their friend through the ceiling and into the room until he was lying at the feet of Jesus. These four men had no ceiling on their faith, and neither will you if you have a God idea! As a result, their friend walked out of that house completely healed.

When people asked the healed man about his miracle, I'm sure he looked at his four friends and shook his head. He knew they were not the brightest bulbs in the lamp, but they had had some desperate faith and God had given them an idea. The man knew how permanent his paralysis had been. The only thing he could say was, "It had to be God."

The Bible says in Psalm 78 that we must tell the younger generations about the miracle-working power of God or they will become stubborn and rebellious. Isn't that what we are seeing in America today? Young people are stubborn and rebellious because they have lost hope in their tomorrows. They are being taught about right and wrong, good and evil, and supernatural power by Harry Potter instead of Moses, David, Paul, and Jesus.

That's why we must demonstrate how only God brings us out of our setbacks into our comebacks and beyond. He alone is the one who really cares, really knows, and really shows! Whether it is a huge miracle like the paralyzed man being healed or a small miracle like getting a great parking space at the grocery store, don't forget to tell the truth: "It had to be God!"

Jump the Facts

Most Christians get too bogged down with the circumstances of their lives. They need to learn how to jump the facts with a God idea. A God idea will always jump the facts because the only way you can carry out a God idea is to have desperate faith that He will perform miracles to get you where you need to go. He plans it that way! He wants to work with you.

How do you think Daniel felt when he was staring at a dozen hungry lions that had been eating people for breakfast, lunch, and dinner (Daniel 6)? He had to jump the facts and believe God would shut their mouths so he could live to fulfill his purpose. That story is probably one of the most famous in the Bible and has been told over and over for thousands of years to give people hope in desperate situations.

God is the same today as He was in the days of Daniel. I recently read about a young woman whose entire life has been jumping the facts. Aimee Mullins is a beautiful, energetic, athlete and fashion model. She has blasted through manmade ceilings to do the impossible all her life. She is a double amputee who says, "The truth is, I'm sort of lucky to have this body, because it forced me to find my strength and beauty within. So, if I don't turn my legs into a big thing, others don't either. And if I let them see who I am inside as well as outside, hopefully they like me for me."[1]

Aimee was born with a deformity that could have kept her bound to a wheelchair. The fibula, one of the major weight-bearing bones in the lower leg, was missing in both of her legs. With great courage, her parents made a decision when she was only one year old to amputate her legs so she could be fitted with prostheses. Aimee literally took her disabilities in stride and was walking by the time she was two. She now has four different pairs of legs: one for everyday use, one for swimming, a special graphite pair for running, and a special cosmetic pair for looks.

Aimee says, "I decided at an early age to transform any setbacks into strengths and tackle them head-on." That's exactly what she has done. In her childhood there was nothing her brothers did that she wouldn't try and master. She swam, played soccer, skied, and had her own paper route. She delivered papers on her bicycle each morning. In college she competed on a Division 1 track team with able-bodied athletes. She became an avid runner and holds two world records in the Paralympics (athletes with disabilities) despite the fact that a double-amputee's body requires three times as much energy and 40 percent more oxygen as a regular body during strenuous exercise.

Aimee never tries to hide who she is or the fact that she is an amputee. Wearing shorts or miniskirts doesn't bother her at all. She uses every opportunity to help others learn to be comfortable with her disabilities. She has co-founded HOPE (Helping Other People Excel), a nonprofit organization that provides training for disabled athletes, and has plans to help amputees get artificial limbs. She says, "Let me be the one who changes fear into understanding and makes people comfortable with amputees. Who knows? Maybe, little by little, I can change the world."

Aimee Mullins' dream to be a fashion model was not just to show her pretty face. She wanted to do runway shows and photo spreads in order to redefine what "beautiful" really meant—and she succeeded. She explains it this way, "As a model I can confront society's emphasis on physical perfection and say, 'Hey, look at me. You think I'm hot, but guess what? I have artificial legs!' There is no ideal body. Mine is very imperfect, and I can't change that — but I can still be attractive. Confidence is the sexiest thing a woman can have. It's much sexier than any body part."

Aimee not only entered the world of modeling, but acting as well. And in 1999 she was named one of *People* magazine's fifty most beautiful people. She doesn't deny the fact that she is an amputee; she has jumped that fact with a positive, unbeatable attitude—and a lot of God ideas. She is sowing seeds of greatness into other people's lives and gains great joy and satisfaction from it.

When Aimee's parents held their baby girl in their arms for the first time, they knew their little girl would be confined to a wheelchair the rest of her life. Their desperate faith opened their minds to a God idea, which led to an entirely different life for their daughter. They jumped the facts, and then their daughter made jumping over facts a way of life!

SHIFT YOUR DISH

I was at a friend's house to watch a football game. He lives out in the country and had just bought a new satellite dish. He was excited and couldn't wait to show it to me. He said, "Tim, watch this. Wherever I shift the dish, that's what I pick up. I can watch games on the East coast, in the Midwest, or anywhere."

It struck me that that is what we need to do. We need to shift our dish to what we want to pick up. We can shift our dish to the, "All Things Are Miserable" Stuck-in-a-Setback Network; or we can shift our dish to the "All Things Are Possible" Miracle Network. When we shift our dish to hear and see what God is saying and doing, we get a miracle mindset that understands the value and power of desperate faith in a God who cares.

When Bill McCartney was getting the vision for Promise Keepers, he would often say, "I may be crazy, but I see stadiums filled with men." He was having a God idea, and he had to raise the ceiling of his expectations, get some desperate faith, and step out into the unknown.

If you have never heard of Promise Keepers, it has become one of the most influential Christian men's organizations in the nation. Stadiums that seat 50,000 have been packed out with men who hold hands in prayer, weep, hug, and encourage each other. Through this organization, men are stepping into their rightful place as leaders in their homes, and their families are being restored. Now it's spreading around the world. I've heard men talking about Promise Keepers in Sweden, Norway, and England. It takes a miracle mindset and desperate faith to accomplish something this powerful.

LET HIM REARRANGE THE FURNITURE

If God is speaking to you about something that seems ridiculous or crazy, don't walk the other way. Shift your dish and jump the facts. You've got a miracle in the making. Start acting and living like the champion you are, the person He created you to be.

When God called me into the healing ministry, I had never seen anybody healed. He also said, "You're going to travel around the world," and at that time I hadn't traveled eighty miles away from home! I had to raise the roof on my expectations. I had to let God rearrange my surroundings and my relationships. It was just like when I moved into a new house, and I had to find a new way to arrange my furniture. Sometimes I had to buy new furniture. God was stretching me and desperate faith grew in me.

To pursue the ministry He had called me to, I had to bring people into my life who had a miracle mentality. Today I still purposely get around people who will stretch me and fire up my faith for miracles.

God is stretching you right now as you read this book. I hope you are having some desperate faith just to believe what you are reading! I pray for that because desperate faith is what is going to open up your mind and heart for an outrageous God idea and all the miracles He wants to do in you, for you, and through you to make that idea a reality. Desperate faith fuels the God ideas— big and small—that will take you out of your setback into your comeback and beyond.

13

IT'S STILL GOING TO
BE ALL RIGHT

"Right now I would really like to believe it's still going to be all right, but something has happened I never thought would happen. I came back from a major setback and did everything I could to keep from having another one. I went beyond my comeback to bigger and better things. All of a sudden, I find myself in this horrible situation and I realize I made some more bad decisions. I know you said that setbacks are part of life, especially if you are trying to do something really good, but I never thought I would wind up in the toilet again! I just don't see how things can get 'all right' again."

Let me begin by telling you a true story that was so important, all the gospel writers included it in their books. It is found in Matthew 26, Mark 14, Luke 22, and John 18. After three-and-a-half years of following Jesus, Peter was a seasoned a veteran. Great things were happening. He was preaching, praying, healing the sick, and casting out demons. He was feeling pretty confident about himself, maybe even a little cocky. It had taken a lot of faith to put down his fishing nets and become a "fisher of men," but that leap of faith had really paid off. Now most people knew that Simon Peter, the rough and uneducated fisherman, was the Messiah's right-hand man.

Simon Peter didn't know that a big dose of reality was just on the horizon. Jesus saw it coming and warned him. He said, "Simon, stay on your toes. Satan has tried his best to separate all of you from me, like chaff from wheat. Simon, I've prayed for you in particular that you not give in or give out. When you have come through the time of testing, turn to your companions and give them a fresh start" (Luke 22:31 MSG).

Peter responded like little Arnold did on the TV show, *Different Strokes*, saying, "Whatchyou talkin' 'bout!" Peter was rugged, strong-willed, passionate, expressive, and overconfident. He never did anything halfway. He was feeling good. He was living large. So when Jesus said Satan was going to come after him, Peter said, "Don't worry about me. Maybe 'doubting' Thomas or that crybaby, John—and I saw Judas stealing from the moneybag. He might do it. But I'll never let You down." Peter's pride and arrogance got in the way of hearing what Jesus was trying to tell him.

Jesus tried again, "I'm sorry to have to tell you this, Peter, but before the rooster crows you will have three times denied that you know me" (Luke 22:34 MSG).

Later that evening soldiers came to arrest Jesus, and what did Peter do? He drew his sword and cut off the right ear of the servant of the chief priest. Jesus reached out and put the man's ear back on. Don't you wonder what the soldiers thought when they saw that miracle, or what they talked about later that night?

At least for that moment, Peter was a loyal follower of Jesus. As the soldiers took Jesus away, however, Peter followed at a *distance*. You don't backslide overnight, you don't gain weight in one meal, and you don't commit adultery or rob a bank on a whim. It takes time. Certain wrong thought processes must be in place.

Peter had always been in the middle of things and out in front, but suddenly he was following at a distance. Before that night was over, he had denied three times that he knew his beloved friend and master, Jesus. When the rooster crowed, he was vehemently cussing and denying he was part of Jesus' group. Just at that moment Jesus looked directly at Peter, as if to say, "I know you failed, but it's still going to be all right." At that moment Peter realized what he had done, and he went outside and wept bitterly.

Peter went from feeling good to feeling ashamed. He was confused, guilty, shocked, and caught in the grip of hopelessness. That's what can happen in life. You find yourself in a situation you never thought you could be in. Sometimes, you have been there before and thought you would never come to that place again. I'm here to tell you that it doesn't matter. It's still going to be all right if you will run to the Refuge.

JESUS' COMEBACK RELEASES ANY COMEBACK

Peter was in a major setback. He thought he had done something unforgiveable. What he didn't realize (because he didn't believe what Jesus said earlier) was that Jesus was also in a major setback. (See Matthew 27-28, Mark 15-16, Luke 23-24, John 19-20.) He was arrested, beaten, and accused by His own people; then He was turned over to the dreaded Roman governor, who whipped Him and ordered Him to be crucified.

Hanging on the cross, Jesus forgave everyone and died. He was buried in a tomb that was sealed and put under Roman guard. I would say that being dead and having your tomb sealed and heavily guarded was a pretty big setback, wouldn't you? Even Houdini couldn't get out of this one! But on the third day after His burial, the greatest comeback in history occurred. Jesus rose from the dead—and that same resurrection power is what makes every comeback we need possible.

Mary Magdalene and other women went to the tomb to anoint Jesus' body with oils and spices, but when they got there they found the large stone had been rolled away from the door. An angel said, "Don't be alarmed. You are looking for Jesus the Nazarene, who was crucified. He has risen! He is not here. See the place where they laid him. But go, tell his disciples *and Peter*" (Mark 16:6-7, italics mine).

This is the only time in Scripture where Jesus actually singles out one person from His team of twelve. We know Jesus had Peter on His mind before He was arrested, but from this we see He had Peter on His mind on the cross (when He forgave all of us), while He was in the grave, and after He rose from the dead. He wanted to be sure Peter knew everything was all right. He wanted to remove that look of failure from his face.

The face tells everything about a person. It is a mirror of your feelings or emotions. You can put makeup on your face. You can have layers burned off with acid or a laser. You can have a facelift or have your lips injected. However, what you are feeling will still show on your face. If you are guilty, it's on your face. If you are sinning, it's on your face. If you are full of shame, it's on your face. Peter's face was totally fallen as he hid in shame.

Suddenly Mary Magdalene burst into the disciples' hiding place and cried, "He's alive! Jesus is alive! He's risen just like He said He would!"

God has a way of shocking us out of our setbacks sometimes, and Peter instantly acted like himself. Without a word, he bolted out of the hiding place and ran with John to the tomb. Peter ran right in and found Jesus' burial clothes and nothing else. Suddenly some of the things Jesus had said came back to him, and a glimmer of hope came into his heart, *If Jesus can come back from this, maybe He can bring me back from what I have done.*

Never underestimate the power of a glimmer of hope! Hope leads to desperate faith, which leads to a miracle. A few days later, Peter was waking up in his fishing boat (John 21). He and some of the other disciples had fished all night and come up with nothing. Suddenly some guy on the beach started yelling, "Throw your net on the right side!"

Since they had nothing to lose, Peter and the others did as they were told. Before they got the nets entirely in the water, fish were jumping into them. That's when the light bulb went on in John's heart. This had happened to them before, and Jesus had been the one who had told them to cast their nets when they had fished all night and caught nothing. John cried, "It is the Lord!"

Without another thought Peter dove into the water and swam to shore as fast as he could. In minutes he stood dripping wet in front of Jesus. Then he remembered how he had denied Him, and he dropped his gaze to His feet. He turned and looked to see the fishing boats coming to shore and ran to help them.

After a great breakfast of fresh fish, Jesus took Peter aside. In what was probably the conversation of Peter's life, Jesus told him what He wanted him to do and even how he would die in serving him. Peter came back. He came back to Jesus and went on to preach the first gospel message on the Day of Pentecost, the day the Church of Jesus Christ was born. Jesus' comeback released Peter's comeback, and Jesus' comeback releases all the comebacks you need too.

JESUS ONLY WRITES HAPPY ENDINGS

I was taking my children to a movie once, and my daughter said, "I'm not going to even go in unless this one has a happy ending. The last one you took me to about the gorillas didn't have a happy ending. This one better have a happy ending!" We all want to know everything is going to turn out all right. Am I going to meet my goals? Will my marriage break out of this rut? Will I lose this weight? Will we ever pay off these debts?

Jesus took Peter's setback and comeback personally, and He takes yours personally too. He knows you want a happy ending because He put that desire in you. He is the author of the book that is called you, and He wants to give you a happy ending. In fact, He doesn't know any other way! That's why they call the Gospel the Good News. Jesus has brought nothing but Good News, and even the prophesies of wars and famine and earthquakes ultimately end with a new Heaven and a new Earth that are perfect.

If we stick with Jesus, we will face some setbacks in our short lives, and some of us will be shocked at the stuff we go through, but our eternal life that lasts forever—no way can our minds get around that! It will be absolutely the most perfect, happy ending. It will be something we can't even imagine. In the meantime, we can look forward to Him making everything all right again and again in this life. What He did for Peter He is still doing for us today.

I was twenty-two years old, preaching at the City Church in Stockholm, Sweden, when an older couple invited me to come to their home in a small village for a rest. I was tired and welcomed time in a little village about eight hours from Stockholm.

When I arrived, I settled into my room in their cozy home and decided to take a nap. In my sleep I heard a voice say, "Get up, get on a bicycle, and ride. You're going to help someone." I wrestled with that voice for awhile because I wanted to sleep, but I knew it was God and forced myself to get up.

I asked the lady who owned the home, "Do you have a bicycle?"

She said, "We have a bicycle, but it is a small bicycle for a young person."

I said, "You don't have a bigger bicycle?"

She said, "No, only the little one. Why do you need a bicycle?"

I said, "I'd like to go for a ride."

She laughed, "Oh, you cannot get on this bicycle. It's too little."

I heard the voice again, "Get on the bike and ride."

I said, "Oh no, I like little bicycles," while I was thinking, *God, why couldn't You get me a bigger bike or a motorcycle?!*

I finally convinced her to lend me the bike, climbed on it, and started down a winding road to an unknown destination. God's man of power! My knees were almost hitting my chin. The front wheel was wobbling back and forth as I tried to keep my balance. As I moved slowly along, however, I had the impression I was supposed to go to a lake.

I saw some people and stopped. I asked them, "Do you have a lake around here?"

They looked at me funny but said, "Oh yes, we have a lake. You go left."

I ignored their stares and followed their directions to the small lake. As soon as I stopped to rest, I heard a voice call out, "Hey, you! Are you from America?"

I yelled back, "Yes!"

It's Still Going to Be All Right

A young man motioned for me to come around to the other side of the lake. As I got closer, I saw he had long hair and a long earring in each ear. He said, "Hey man. You like rock 'n roll?"

I was thinking, *God, You woke me up for this?* I was a little cranky when I answered, "No. I don't like rock 'n roll."

He said, "I do. I'm a rock 'n roll kind of guy. I love the Rolling Stones."

Now I thought maybe it wasn't God I had heard. Maybe it was all that sausage I had had for dinner last night.

He said, "What are you doing here in this dead village, man?"

"I'm here resting."

He asked, "What do you do?"

My attitude was going downhill fast, and rather sarcastically I said, "I'm a minister. You know, a bringer of *Good News.*"

That's when he screamed, "Ahhhh!"

I said, "What's your problem?"

He said, "I'm a backslidder."

I really didn't care by now and corrected him, "A backslider."

He said, "Yeah. Well, I'm a drug addict. I used to serve God."

I said, "Well, I'm a preacher." Then I began to talk to him, and as I talked, God began to get *my* attention. His power began to flow through me, and I was suddenly grateful. My attitude was changed when I asked him, "What do you want to do?"

He said, "I wanta, I wanta come back to Jesus."

I saw this little chain around his neck inside his shirt and said, "Let me see what's in there." He pulled it out, and it was an upside down cross, which is a satanic cross. I said, "Get rid of that," and he immediately threw it in the lake. Then he threw his beer and cigarettes in the trash can and got down on his knees without me even asking him to do it. I got off my little bike, laid my hands on him, and began to pray. The resurrecting power of God shook him, and he began to weep. Then I began to weep. I didn't care if I was riding a kiddy bike. I didn't care what I looked like, how tired I was, or who was staring at me. Jesus was there.

The boy got to his feet and said, "Now, we must tell my mother-in-law. She's afraid of me. I'm mean to my wife. I'm a bad man. I mean really bad. I must tell her what's happened. The house is right over there."

I have preached in some of the greatest churches in the world, but what happened next was one of the all-time high points of my ministry. It showed me how much Jesus cares that we get a happy ending. No matter what we have done or how many times we fall, it's still going to be all right!

The mother-in-law took one look at me and started screaming, "Tim Storey! Tim Storey! Tim Storey!" I froze in my tracks. I was a young minister and not many people knew who I was. I'd never been in this town, which was a day's drive from Stockholm and the church where I had preached.

The boy hugged his wife, hugged his mother-in-law, and they were all talking in Swedish and crying. They started twirling each other around in the living room. I was standing there trying to take it all in. Finally, the mother-in-law told me in English, "This is what happened. I was visiting my sister in Stockholm for a few days. I was at City Church sitting in the back row of the balcony when you were there. As you were preaching I said, 'God, send a man like Tim Storey to set my son-in-law free.'"

If you have ever been close to a drug addict, and a mean, abusive one at that, you know how much you need a miracle. Only desperate faith comes through in a situation like that, and when that boy's mother-in-law prayed, I believe Jesus heard and immediately went into action. He whispered to that older couple to invite me for a rest in their home. He interrupted my nap and told me to get on a bike and take a ride. He told me to find a lake, and then He gave me favor with the young man because I was a young American.

Jesus made all this happen to free that young man from drugs, to restore him to his family, and to give young Tim Storey another experience proving that God has a comeback for everyone, no matter how low they have sunk or how many times they have fallen.

Your Challenges

God knows exactly where you are, and He doesn't care if it's the third, fourth, or eightieth time you have fallen down. He can lift you out of your setback just like He lifted Peter and that young man in Sweden. Once you believe that, however, you should realize that there are going to be thoughts and emotions that will come against you to try to stop you.

Three things that will sabotage your comeback are self-pity, pride, and condemnation. Self-pity says, "If you were going through what I'm going through, you wouldn't be singin' and dancin' either." Self-pity is nursed, cursed, and rehearsed over and over. You nurse it by feeling sorry for yourself and thinking *poor me*. Self-pity is all about self. You are elevating yourself above everyone else because nobody suffers like you suffer!

Then you utter curses of self-pity by saying things like, "My whole family are alcoholics and drug addicts. My father was always in debt. My mother was always sick. I wouldn't be this way if it wasn't for them. It's all their fault." You rehearse self-pity by playing the videos of past mistakes over and over in your mind. The more you think about it, the more you feel sorry for yourself.

Pride is also wrapped up in self. Maybe you can relate to Peter, who just couldn't believe he was capable of denying Jesus and running like a coward. He thought he was above fear, betrayal, and self-centeredness. He was so quick to say, "Not me! I'll never deny you, Lord." I travel all over the world, and I can't tell you how many times I have heard people say, "I didn't think I would do it or even could do it, but I did."

God always tells us the truth about ourselves, and He says that we are all capable of all kinds of terrible things.

If we claim that we're free of sin, we're only fooling ourselves. A claim like that is errant nonsense. On the other hand, if we admit our sins—make a clean breast of them—he won't let us down; he'll be true to himself. He'll forgive our sins and purge us of all wrongdoing.

—1 John 1:8-9 MSG

Be quick to admit when you are wrong and when you have sinned against God and other people. And don't ever believe you are above doing it again! If you have this realistic understanding of yourself, you will stick close to Jesus. *It's when Peter lagged behind and hid that he fell.* If you stay close to Jesus and other believers, you will stay humble and pride will not hold you back. You will also stay free of condemnation. This is a great tool of the enemy, who will sit on your shoulder and tell you, "You've really done it now! No one will ever trust you again. Your family doesn't even believe what you say. There's no hope and no future for you."

Do you know why that statement is a total lie? It is a lie because Jesus forgives everything. He didn't die and shed His sinless blood so you could drown in condemnation the rest of your life. He sacrificed Himself for you so that you could be forgiven and walk free of your past sins—all of them.

Every time you mess up, I'm sure you go through the condemnation dirty laundry list: I could've, should've, and if only I would've. If only I'd stayed in college, I could've been a doctor by now. I should've listened to my parents and made better choices for friends. I wish I would've stayed away from those wild parties.

Just because you are in a setback doesn't mean your dream is dead! You can be forgiven, get fresh insight, and move forward—which is your next challenge. You have got to show up! Suppose Peter had received forgiveness and decided he was content to catch fish the rest of his life? What if he didn't want to take the chance that he would fail Jesus again? Fish were a sure bet, so he would skip the Upper Room—and then he never would have come back. Proof of Peter's comeback was when he showed up to preach the sermon of his life and led three thousand Jews to their Messiah on the Day of Pentecost.

Even when you're in the middle of a setback and don't feel like it, force yourself to get out of bed. Take a shower, brush your teeth, put on clean clothes, turn off the TV, and talk to Jesus. Ask Him what you need to do at that moment to move toward your comeback. It might be something as small as making your bed and cleaning your room, or it might be something big like booking a hotel for a conference. Take a deep breath and thank God you're alive if nothing else seems right. But get up, show up, and cooperate with the comeback He has for you.

TURN THE CORNER

You never know what God has planned for you just around the corner, so you have to turn some corners to find out. A corner means a change of direction. Every day you pass corners around furniture, along city streets, in office hallways, and even taking a walk in the woods. After you make a turn, sometimes you are greeted with the unexpected.

That's what happened to Mary. She was planning her wedding to Joseph and was excited to begin a new life with him. He was a good man. Then the angel Gabriel showed up and told her, "Mary, you need to turn a corner." The corner Mary agreed to turn changed the lives of every human being. She was a young teenager, a nobody, but God chose her to bear His Son.

When you are in a setback, turning a corner can be frightening or exhilarating. Turning a corner might bring you to more persecution and ridicule, or it might bring you to a new job, a fun relationship, or an opportunity to help someone who is in even worse shape than you are in. One thing is certain: If you are turning the corner God wants you to turn, no matter what is on the other side He will use it for your good. He will use it for your comeback.

In John, chapter 11, some of Jesus' closest friends were asked to turn a hard corner, and it resulted in a major miracle. Lazarus and his sisters, Mary and Martha, lived in Bethany, just outside Jerusalem, and Jesus loved to visit them. One day when Jesus was ministering in the wilderness where John the Baptist used to baptize people in the Jordan River, word came to Him that Lazarus was sick and on the verge of death. Lazarus' sisters wanted Him to come immediately.

Jesus sent word that Lazarus' sickness would not end in death. The messenger returned to Mary and Martha singing, "I got a feeling everything's gonna be all right!" I'm sure they thought Jesus would arrive soon after, but Lazarus died, was buried, and had been dead four days before He got there!

Everyone was grieving and crying, but Jesus had a reason for waiting. The Jews believed that the spirit of a dead person hovered over the grave for three days, and in that three days he might come back. After three days, however, it was completely impossible for someone to be raised from the dead.

Isn't it just like God to wait until something is completely impossible in human culture and reasoning before He brings a breakthrough? The more I walk with Him, the more I understand that with God it's never too late. No matter what has happened, it's still going to be all right.

Jesus arrived and saw Martha first. She was really angry and said, "If you had been here on time, Lazarus wouldn't be dead!"

Jesus said, "He will rise again," and she thought He was referring to the time when all dead saints would be resurrected. But Jesus continued, "I am the resurrection and the life. He who believes in me will live, even though he dies; and whoever lives and believes in me will never die. Do you believe this?" (John 11:25, 26).

Martha suddenly caught on! She turned a corner in faith and said, "Yes, Lord." She went to get Mary, who was still having a pity party. Mary met Jesus with the same accusation, "Jesus, if You had been here, my brother wouldn't have died." Then something very interesting happened. It's the shortest verse in the Bible but it is one of the most powerful. It says, "Jesus wept" (John 11:35).

Even though He knew He was going to raise Lazarus from the dead, Jesus wept because He felt their pain. Don't ever buy the lie that God has forsaken you and Jesus is standing there, arms folded, too "holy" and "together" to feel what you are feeling. No! He is right in there with you! He is holy and together, but He's also human. He identifies with you; and when you understand that, you can identify with Him. That is turning a big corner!

Despite Mary's unbelief, Martha still believed they were about to see the resurrection power of God in action. She turned that corner of faith—and they did! Jesus raised Lazarus from the dead.

If Jesus can raise people from the dead, He can raise your dreams from the dead. It's still going to be all right, no matter what people say and no matter what the circumstances. Resurrection power raised Lazarus from the dead, raised Jesus from the dead, made Peter into the great man of God we know about today, and restored an abusive drug addict to his family and his right mind. That same resurrection power is working in your life right now. Be like Martha and just believe it! Turn the corner, and you will see the miracle that God has waiting for you.

14

YOU CAN BE GREAT

"To be blunt, from what I've been reading, I feel like if I don't do something really big in my life, if I don't become rich or famous or both, my life won't count for much. You talk about the history-maker and world-changer, and I just don't identify with that at all. Maybe I would have years ago, when I was a teenager and thought I would be Indiana Jones or Luke Skywalker one day, but my life has turned out completely different from what I thought it would be. My life is okay, but you wouldn't write a book about it or make a movie out of it or anything."

What you are talking about is what I call the Hollywood mentality, and that can be good or bad. Hollywood has probably made more of an impact on generations of young people in America than any other industry. The movies we watch as we grow up subtly define who we are and what we aspire to be in life. You watched Indiana Jones and Luke Skywalker and maybe you wanted to be a top gun fighter pilot, a SWAT team policeman, or an oceanic explorer. The point is, those characters inspired you to live a heroic life.

Unfortunately, there are other kinds of movies that inspire much less heroic lives. Some kids got hooked on vampire movies and horror flicks and got into the Gothic movement. Their lives became dark shadows, just like the famous soap opera years ago, only it's not funny. Some in my generation saw *Animal House* and *Easy Rider* and moved into the world of sex and drugs and complete irresponsibility, thinking that was the cool thing to do. Their lives were defined by, "If it feels good do it." They became parents and now they don't understand why their kids are in and out of drug rehab, relationships, and jobs.

Through the years, I have seen and talked to hundreds of young kids who are walking the streets of LA as prostitutes and drug addicts. They came to Hollywood to become rich and famous in the movies. If there is any place that illustrates that "all that glitters is not gold," it is Hollywood! Unfortunately, there are still so many who are waiting for their big break, and they think that one big break is going to make their lives perfect. Just talk to someone like Robert Downey Jr., and you will find out that getting that big break and becoming rich and famous does not guarantee self-respect, satisfaction, or happiness. Then go on the Internet and look up how many young "stars" have died of drug overdoses or suicide in the last ten years.

"Okay, I see your point, but what about those who have made it in the business world or in education or sports? There are a lot of rich and famous people who are not in Hollywood."

You Can Be Great

You have been blunt with me, and now I'm going to be blunt with you. As a whole, our society has become celebrity obsessed, and I believe the enemy is using that to cause people who are making a difference in their world to feel like their lives are insignificant, unimportant, and even worthless. Most of the world never heard of my mother, but she sure made all the difference in the lives of her children! To us kids, she is a world-changer and a history-maker. I can give you so many examples of people you never heard of who have made a huge difference in my life. I'm sure you can think of examples in your life as well.

The world is made up of all kinds of people—tall and short, chubby and skinny, different colors, cool and not so cool. Some are famous, some are wealthy, and some are poor and unnoticed; but most people are right in the middle. What I see again and again, no matter who I talk to and what kind of life they have, is that there is one thing all of us need: a relationship with the One who made us and understands us better than anyone else.

True Greatness

Let me tell you the bottom line of all of this: It's not what people say about you that counts; when all is said and done, it is what God says about you that counts. He has designed life so that your life will affect others, whether you think it does or not. Your life is like that stone you throw in the pond. Whether you skip that rock or just throw it as far as you can, it will send out ripples that never stop until they hit the shore. Even the shore is affected!

Did you know that even if you live in a cave and never talk to anyone, you are sending out ripples to those who are connected to you? When you die, what you have done on this Earth will still affect the generations that come after you, whether they are your own children and children's children or someone else's. There is no human being who ever lived that was not important and significant. Why? God loves us all.

God has put in each one of us a desire to be great because He is great. We are His kids, so we are going to want to be great like Him. The problem is, we have allowed the world to define greatness when only God can. He loves us all but made us unique. He loves variety, diversity, and color! What makes me great is not what makes you great. Your greatness will be expressed and revealed as you live the life God has destined you to live. If I try to live my life like you live yours, I will never be great.

When people get celebrity obsessed, they buy into the world's idea of what it means to be great. The businessman can think that if he is not living like Donald Trump, he is not successful. The homemaker and mother can think if she is not a combination of Martha Stewart and Mother Teresa, she is not making a difference. The baseball player who never makes it to the major leagues or makes it but never wins the World Series can believe he is a total failure.

One of the ways I tackle this hideous lie that makes people believe and feel they are unsuccessful and insignificant is to break it down. Life is not an either/or proposition. You are not always wonderful or always terrible. You are not born to be great or born to be a failure. Life is also not based on one big break, and if you don't get that break, your life has no value. No! Life is a series of setbacks and comebacks that, when we let Him, God will use to make us into the person we were created to be and accomplish what we were created to do. Anyone who sticks with Him and follows the path He designed for them will become great!

Being on the news or an entertainment show does not make you a history-maker and a world-shaker; being who you were created to be and doing what you were created to do makes you great.

Follow the Yellow Brick Road

In *The Wizard of Oz,* Dorothy is lost in a foreign land and the Munchkins who live there tell her she must follow the yellow brick road to get back home. The yellow brick road will take her to the Wizard, who will tell her how to go home. Think about it. What made that movie interesting was everything Dorothy experienced and all the creatures she met while she traveled that road. If she had gone straight from her house to the Wizard and then home, there would have been no setbacks and no comebacks. It's the setbacks and comebacks that make our lives unique, colorful, and worth living.

It's the setbacks and comebacks that give us the opportunity to develop into the person we were created to be by connecting with the people around us in the right way. Dorothy's big accomplishment was not getting home to Kansas. She changed her world by staying on the yellow brick road and helping everyone she met as she traveled that road.

She got someone who didn't think they had a brain in their head to realize they were a thinker. She helped a person who had a hard, rusted heart to feel love again. She showed a coward that he wasn't a coward after all. And she learned a great deal about herself in the process of helping others in her journey. She found out that the home she had always thought to be common and unsophisticated was filled with the love, security, and wisdom she needed.

Dorothy had to stay on the yellow brick road for all these things to happen, and we have to stay on the path God has for us. Then we will meet the people who will change our lives for the better, who will challenge us to grow up, and who will encourage us to be ourselves and fulfill our purpose. These are also the people we will help, encourage, and challenge to grow up.

We have to contend with life while we are living it, and following God's path for us isn't always easy! That's why God loves to use the least likely people to perform great exploits. It gives the rest of us hope that we can reach our potential and do great things too. He also assures us that "great things" is different for every individual.

You may be traveling along, waiting for your big break in life, wondering when it will ever come. You may be just surviving and getting through another day. What I'm challenging you to do is to stop looking for that one big break and realize there are a lot of breaks coming your way. Stop just surviving and begin to thrive in the place you find yourself.

Your life isn't about a big break; it's about one significant, life-transforming step at a time.

The path God wants you to follow is a path of faithfulness, humility, and trust in Him that as you prosper where you are planted, He will see to it that you accomplish everything you have in your heart to accomplish. Just like Dorothy, you have to follow the path to discover all the things He wants you to discover about yourself, about those around you, and about the world you are impacting as you move forward.

On His path for you, you will encounter good and evil—in yourself as well as others! Also like Dorothy, you will have to get rid of the evil in yourself, pray for those who are acting evil around you, and never stop making your way home by doing the right thing. Ultimately, you will be home forever with your Father in Heaven, a place that will make the Emerald City look shabby! In the meantime, you must follow the path He has laid out for you.

Big Waves Begin With a Little Shift

The world is experiencing great earthquakes today, and being raised in California, I know about earthquakes! They are caused by a small shift deep within the Earth. What we are seeing more and more today are the huge waves that are formed after a small shift and earthquake. Even in nature, God reveals that the smallest of acts has ripple effects in far away places and through time and generations.

In *The Wizard of Oz,* Dorothy had to overcome her fear of the Wicked Witch, and eventually she inadvertently destroyed her. That one little act freed the entire Land of Oz from a terrible evil presence. Now let's get real. Remember Ananias? He was the guy Jesus sent to talk to Saul of Tarsus, who became the apostle Paul. At the time Ananias went to see Saul, however, Saul was still famous for persecuting and killing Christians. No believer in their right mind would have approached him, but that just happened to be one of Ananias' big assignments as he followed the path God had laid out for him.

Ananias isn't famous today. He doesn't end up in Hebrews, chapter 11, where most of the great heroes of the faith are named. Nobody made a movie about his life; but when he overcame his fear and went to pray for Saul of Tarsus, he changed the world. Ananias made a little, tiny shift that caused an earthquake of revelation and sent tidal waves of miracles around the world and to future generations through the acts and writings of the apostle Paul.

Never underestimate the little things God asks you to do!

Whether you are the janitor or the CEO, whether you are the groomsman or the jockey, whether you are in the chorus or the leading lady, know that if you are following the path God has laid out for you, you are making little shifts that are impacting everyone around you.

Every little *thing you do is just as significant as the* big *things you do!*

Help someone where you are, stir up their gift, and you may change history. That young man working beside you at the hardware store may be the next Bill Gates or Sally Ride. Remember when Paul and Silas were locked up in the darkest dungeon in Philippi? They made a small shift. They began to pray and praise God, and a literal earthquake occurred. As a result the jailer came to know Jesus, his family and servants came to know Jesus, and their influence in the city of Philippi brought many more to know Jesus.

When you step out in faith to act on a God idea, mighty miracles happen!

Too many times we become so "I" centered, waiting for our big break, that we are blinded to the opportunities God has placed right in front of us. It's time to think big in small places. What you make happen for someone else, God will make happen for you. When you open a door for someone else to succeed, you are planting a seed into your own success. That seed will germinate and grow with each word of encouragement, with each helping hand you extend. In other words, don't wait for *your* ship to come in if you haven't sent *someone else's* out!

Several years ago my friends Vince Evans and Napoleon McCallum, who were playing for the Oakland Raiders, said, "Tim, we need to start a Bible study for the Raiders." So we started one on Mondays. The first Monday, sixteen guys showed up, and they didn't look like they wanted to be there! Their expressions said, "Vince dragged us in here, so let's get this over with."

I sucked in my gut and decided to act like everyone couldn't wait to hear what I had to say. I began, "Okay, everybody stand up. This is going to be great."

Two guys stood.

I took a deep breath and continued, and the more I talked the more I felt the presence of God on me and on them. Then things began to happen. Those guys who wouldn't stand up the first time were standing and clapping and cheering. They dragged their friends to our next meeting. Before long we had about thirty players at this non-mandatory Bible study on Monday morning, and the whole team began to change!

It only takes one person to make a difference. Just one little shift, an earthquake shakes people, and a tidal wave of God's love and power falls on them. Now say this out loud, "I happen to be the one!" If you are willing, God can use you to make big waves. You can be great—whether or not people know your name!

TIMING IS EVERYTHING

There are different times and seasons in your life. There is a season for a setback and a season for a comeback. There is a time for grieving and a time for rejoicing; a time to work and time to play. Life is like the ebb and flow of the tides in the ocean. Again, you are always changing and moving forward if you are on the path God has for you, but there are principles and truths that never change. He has given you these to hold you steady as you experience all the different seasons of your life.

There is also a time to plant and a time to harvest. You cannot go out in the fields and pick an ear of corn five days after you plant the corn seed. You must go through the God-ordained process of weeding, fertilizing, watering, and waiting while the sun and all the God-ordained elements work to grow that corn to maturity.

There was a guy in the Bible named Joseph (you can read his story in Genesis, chapters 37, 39-45) who had two dreams when he was a teenager. His family called him "The Dreamer," but they didn't mean it in a good way. They were angry because these dreams showed that one day the whole family, even his mother and father, would bow down to Joseph—and he was one of the youngest of the children!

Unfortunately for Joseph, he thought the season for his dreams to come to pass was right away, but the dreams were simply the seeds for his future. God was planting those seeds in his heart, but it would be a long time and he would go through a lot of seasons of growth before those dreams would reach maturity.

Joseph either didn't know or he forgot about God's timing. When he shared those dreams with his family, they thought he was a boastful little brat. His brothers threw him in a pit and then sold him as a slave to a group of wandering traders. He ended up in Egypt, a slave to Potiphar, who was a wealthy captain in Pharaoh's army. It wasn't long before Potiphar recognized God's favor upon Joseph. He knew this because Joseph did everything well and everything he did turned out great, so he made Joseph overseer of his entire household.

One thing you are going to see again and again about Joseph: Even though he went through some terrible setbacks, he always kept his faith in God and worked hard to come back. He never gave up on God or the dreams God had given him as a boy. He went through many setbacks and comebacks before the dreams came to pass—and by then he was mature enough to handle his success.

Everything was going well at Potiphar's house until his wife made a sexual advance toward Joseph. He refused her and fled, which really made her mad! Her anger landed Joseph in prison, falsely accused of attacking her. Again, the prison warden soon saw God's favor on Joseph as he faithfully carried out small tasks. Eventually he set Joseph in a place of great authority in the prison.

Wherever Joseph was, the Lord promoted him because he kept the faith and was faithful to do excellent work wherever he was. He didn't bad-mouth those he worked for, he didn't complain when things were unfair or difficult, and he didn't try to get ahead by putting anyone else down. He just served everyone like he was serving God himself. I'm sure this wasn't easy at times! Joseph was as human as you and me, but overall he did the right thing.

One day, Pharaoh's baker and butler were thrown into prison and placed under Joseph's supervision. They each had a dream, and God gave Joseph the meaning for each dream. Just as Joseph had told them, the baker was hanged but the butler was released from prison and restored to his position in Pharaoh's court. The butler forgot about Joseph until two years later, when Pharaoh had a dream. None of Pharaoh's magicians and holy men could interpret it, so the butler recommended Joseph.

Joseph was brought from the prison, cleaned up, and taken before Pharaoh to interpret his dream. He continually gave God credit for his gift, so God showed Joseph the meaning of Pharaoh's dream and Joseph explained to Pharaoh that there would be seven years of plenty and then seven years of famine in the land. God then gave Joseph a plan to prepare for the time of famine.

Pharaoh also recognized the Spirit of God was on Joseph, so he appointed him to rule over his kingdom. He said, "Only with respect to the throne will I be greater than you" (Genesis 41:40).

Suddenly Joseph had all of Egypt bowing to him, but what about his family? When the famine hit Israel, Joseph's father sent his brothers to Egypt to buy supplies. They bowed before Joseph, not knowing who he was! Then Joseph gave them supplies and had them bring back his father and the one brother who wasn't with them. He was able to save their lives by bringing them to Egypt. By this time his mother was dead, but everyone in the family bowed to Joseph, and the dreams he had had as a young man were fulfilled.

Joseph went from the pit, to the prison, to the palace, but wherever he was in his journey he prospered because he was faithful and full of faith. He respected the authority under which he found himself and allowed the Spirit of God to shine in his life. He kept his attitude right and didn't seek vengeance on those who caused him harm. Joseph poured himself into other people's lives. He was a man of integrity and purpose, and God used him to preserve his family, the family that would eventually bring forth the Messiah Jesus!

There is always a process to go through before a dream comes into fullness, and the more you are aware of God's timing, the easier the process will be. That process always includes tests and trials, learning self-discipline, humility, and growing in wisdom and discernment. The pit, the slave master, and the prison are all training grounds for the palace.

To be great, you must understand the importance of God's timing.

Growth and maturity are necessary for you to successfully handle the comeback God has for you. He knows the right time for everything. He knows when you will be ready and when you won't. You may not think you are ready at times, but He will. Sometimes you will think you are more than ready, and still He holds you back. Take it from someone who has experienced this again and again—you can trust Him to get you to the right place at the right time!

DIAMONDS IN SOUTH AFRICA

I was playing golf in South Africa, which is famous for its diamond fields, and I found diamonds in an unusual place. You have never seen the diamonds glitter on the shopping channels or the Internet sites, but they are shining their light in significant places nonetheless.

As we played golf, I didn't like the way the black caddies were treated. Instead of getting all judgmental and critical of those who were mistreating them, I decided to motivate the caddies to rise above it. One of them, named Steven, was complaining. I said, "Steven, who are you going to help by feeling sorry for yourself?"

He said, "Well, that's easy for you to say. You're from America."

I answered, "You're probably right, but we need to prosper where we are planted right now or we are never going to change our situation." Steven was totally unkempt. He had a big Afro with grass all over it and his clothes were ragged. I knew that if he didn't change on the inside, changing the outside wouldn't help him; but helping him to change on the outside would open the door for the powerful message I had for him to change him on the inside.

I said, "Steven, I'm not putting you down, but we're going to have to do something about you. What time do you get off tomorrow?" He told me what time, and I met him and some others the next day. I took them shopping and bought them some nice clothes and shoes, got them haircuts, and gave them some motivational tapes that talked about God. Then I said, "Now, you guys are going to make a shift in the way you are living, because if you don't act right, your children are not going to act right, and then your children's children are going to be messed up. But you are going to make some little changes that are going to cause some big turnarounds for your families and your community."

I knew that if I just gave them a pep talk, they would write me off. The only way they would listen is if I did something for them that showed I really cared. I had to put my money where my mouth was. These caddies couldn't believe somebody cared enough about them to buy them new clothes and get them haircuts. They were so excited. Three days later I went back to play golf, and they were wearing their new clothes and shoes. They were struttin' around like they owned the place!

That was several years ago, and Steven now runs his own business. He's still looking sharp, and the people around him are looking sharp. That one shopping trip and the words of encouragement shared gave him a new start, a new heart, and a new life because someone showed concern about a young caddie. It only takes one person! I shifted, he shifted, and suddenly an entire family moved from poverty to security, from complaining to being thankful, from spinning their wheels to racing down the track.

That's how little people make big waves. It doesn't happen by standing around waiting for the big break. It happens by putting your hope and trust in a relevant, reliable, credible God, because He has your future already prepared. It happens by reaching out and helping somebody else obtain their dream, by finding and polishing those diamonds in the rough.

GOD LOOKS FOR A SMALL FRY

Do you know how I am usually introduced to the famous people I have helped through the years? It's the nanny or the gardener or the maid. These are the people who love Jesus and serve their employers well because that is the same as serving Jesus well. Everything they do, they do it like they were doing it for Jesus. Because they serve so well, their employers listen when they say, "You know, I know a minister who might help you to get through this. He's helped a lot of people you might know."

There's a story in the Old Testament just like this, found in the book of 2 Kings, chapter 5, about a man called Naaman. He was the army commander for the king of Syria, and he got leprosy. It just so happened that one of his servant girls was from Israel. She told Naaman there was a prophet in Israel named Elisha, who could heal people.

Naaman knew this servant girl was honest, so he went to Israel to see Elisha. Because he was a big shot, he was furious when Elisha didn't come out to speak to him directly. Instead, Elisha sent a servant to tell him to dip in the Jordan River seven times and he would be healed. Again, it was Naaman's servants who convinced him to obey Elisha's instructions. When Naaman humbled himself and did what he was told to do, the leprosy disappeared. As a result, this mighty Syrian warrior chose to follow the one true God, and he carried his new faith back to Syria.

One little servant girl impacted a nation.

BEING GREAT IS A CHOICE

There's something about setbacks that make us want to take it out on everyone around us. When we feel bad, we want everyone else to feel bad. That is exactly the opposite of what we should be doing. To go from a setback to a comeback and beyond, we have to find the path God has for us, or at least the first step, and take it. We have to look beyond our own situation and remember that other people in our lives have problems too.

Let's go back once again to Dorothy in *The Wizard of Oz*. She held onto her dog, Toto, because he represented everything she loved and believed was right. She was in a terrible setback, but when she met the Scarecrow, the Tin Man, and the Cowardly Lion she didn't take it out on them. She helped them, and by helping them she moved toward both her goal and becoming a great heroine.

These are the things that make Dorothy great: She decided to care for others in the midst of her own setback, she chose to stay on the yellow brick road until she got her comeback, and she went beyond her comeback by choosing to be herself. She didn't try to be anyone else. She didn't try to be the next good witch or try to take the Wizard's place when he turned out to be less than everybody said he was. And she was honest about her own fears and faults. In the end, she found peace in who she was and what she was to do.

True greatness is knowing on the inside of you that you are being true to who God made you to be on the outside. I can sense if you are faking it or deceiving yourself, and so can other people. You may be the greatest actor who ever lived and can play any character on this planet, but if you can't be yourself you will never be great.

You Can Be Great

True greatness comes from the inside because God lives in you.

You are going to have setbacks, but God has a comeback for each one. Then you decide if you want to really go beyond the comeback and be great. You can be great. You can serve the God who blesses you and guides you with all your heart, you can care about others, and you can dare to be yourself!

15

A Final Word

God has marked out an adventure for you called life.

He doesn't *cause* anything bad to happen to you, but He is there to miraculously see you through when it does. He knows the world you live in is filled with pitfalls and evil, and He knows you are not perfect and can get yourself in a bind. He knows you are going to have to go through some difficult and sometimes tragic situations. There will be setbacks, but they don't have to be the death of your dreams or the end of a life worth living.

Setbacks can be frustrating, frightening, and debilitating; but never forget that you have a Refuge! At times the road you are walking may seem too steep to climb, too slippery to maintain your footing, or too far to travel; but He is there, and He also walked an excruciatingly painful road to a place called Calvary. I'm sure there were moments when He wondered if He could take the next step. When they nailed Him to the cross, He had to fight for every breath—especially the one that said, "Father, forgive them."

You have an Advocate, a Comforter, a Mentor, a Guide, a Teacher and Trainer who knows your life better than you do, better than your parents or friends or any other human being. He feels your pain when you are hurt and dances with joy when you achieve success. He's with you every step of the way, giving you the strength and wisdom you need to take that next step of faith. Sometimes, you can actually feel Him carrying you when you can't go any further and holding you when your heart is shattered.

He knows what's ahead of you and can prepare you for what's coming. He may tell you to do some crazy things you don't understand and maybe will not understand until you get to Heaven, but you know He knows what's best. He loves you and always wants what is best for you.

After awhile of walking with Him, you will realize what I have realized: Your destination is not only a place but a new way of looking at life. You can embrace the adventure of faith instead of fearing it because His love for you and His power that works on your behalf is so much greater than anything or anyone that tries to hurt or hinder you. I like the way the apostle John said it in his first letter (1 John 4:4): "The one who is in you is greater than the one who is in the world."

You have an enemy in this world, and he is real. His priority is to try to push you off your yellow brick road, to get you to give up before you can help the people you are supposed to help, discover who you really are, and reach your destination. But you also have a God who is greater than lions and tigers and bears—or wicked witches (I'm serious)! He is greater than anything the enemy can throw at you. If you could see how He is defending you and keeping you safe, you would be shocked.

There is a short story in the Old Testament that illustrates this perfectly. The prophet Elisha's servant got up one morning and walked out to find an enemy army of three thousand surrounding Elisha's house and the entire city. He panicked and ran in to tell Elisha, who just yawned and said, "Don't be afraid. Our army is greater than their army." As Elisha turned over to go back to sleep, he prayed, "God, please open his eyes!"

The servant frowned at Elisha and then gasped at what he saw. "He looked and saw the hills full of horses and chariots of fire all around Elisha" (2 Kings 6:17)! Surrounding the enemy army was the angelic host of Heaven, far more powerful than any human army. That's what you have to remember when life feels like two against three thousand trained killers. You have to remember the whole picture, the spiritual reality: There are more with you than with your enemies!

The more you walk with God, the more you will see your life and the lives of others through His eyes of unconditional love and benevolent power. No matter what you face, if you remember how great He is and how much He cares about you and those around you, you won't allow your circumstances to blind you from seeing His supernatural solution.

Isiah Robertson played football for the Los Angeles Rams and the Buffalo Bills, and he was a six-time All Pro. I think he was one of the greatest linebackers of all time. When I was a kid, I loved watching Number 58 play. Then all the glitz and power of living in the fast lane took Isiah from the top to the bottom in life. Drugs got a hold on Him and he lost everything he had.

When he hit bottom, a little ray of hope hit him. He knew it was the God his mother had told him about, and he turned his life over to Him. Gradually, one tiny step at a time, Isiah found his way back to the yellow brick road. He went from his setback to a comeback—and then, because he was finally being who he was created to be, he went beyond.

Isiah built a drug and alcohol rehabilitation home for men, and they have graduated hundreds of young champions out of that place.

Isiah was never alone. When he was in the pit, he grabbed hold of the hand of God, let Him pull him out, and has never let go. Like so many of us, he continues to face setbacks, but with new eyes. He looks to the comebacks, knowing God has already prepared it for him. And he is going beyond by becoming fully himself.

THE SONG OF LOVE

When my son Isaiah was small, he really liked Sony Play Station games, especially the football and basketball games. I have a friend who works for Sony, so he gave me the Play Station games whenever he could. I came home one day with a bag of new games and said, "Isaiah, you've been blessed again!"

He was so excited, he said, "Dad, what'd you get? What'd you get this time?"

I said, "Oh, I think there's at least one blessing in this bag. Let me just see what I've got." Although there were eight games in the bag, I acted like I only had one, pulled one out, and said, "Whoa, look at this."

Isaiah jumped up and down yelling, "Cool, that's just what I wanted!"

I strung out the suspense, slowly pulling out one game after another. With each game he got more and more excited. Finally he ran around the room in his pajamas, laughing, "No, no, no, no! That's too much! Stop! That's too much!"

That's the way your heavenly Father wants to bless you!

You are the love of His life, and He wants to give and give until you're crying, "Stop! I can't take the blessings anymore! I don't even know how to respond! I'm not used to being this happy!" He wants to bless you in the setback, give you a miraculous comeback, and take you way beyond anything you can think or imagine.

The LORD your God is with you, he is mighty to save. he will take great delight in you, he will quiet you with his love, he will rejoice over you with singing.

—Zephaniah 3:17

Imagine that! God is so filled with the joy of knowing you that He is composing songs and singing about you! He is always with you, He is always moving in supernatural, miraculous ways to save you from whatever difficult or perilous situation you are in. He likes you just the way you are! And He will quiet the storms in your life with His love. This verse of Scripture is His promise for you today. He will take you out of your setback, into your comeback, and beyond. So grab onto Him and don't let go!

ABOUT THE AUTHOR

Tim Storey is an acclaimed speaker, writer, and life coach. He is well-known for his radio and television broadcasts and has inspired and motivated people of all walks of life, from entertainment-industry executives, celebrities, and athletes to adults and children in the most deprived neighborhoods in the country. Since receiving his doctorate of divinity from Bethany Theological Seminary, Tim Storey has visited fifty-five countries and spoken to millions of people. He is the author of several books and monographs, notably his 2008 release *Utmost Living*.

To contact Tim Storey, write:

Storey Dreams

499 N. Canon Dr., Suite 400

Beverly Hills, California 90210

www.timstoreyonline.com

ENDNOTES

CHAPTER 1

[1]Definition for "momentum" found at http://www.merriamwebster.com/dictionary/momentum Web. 26 April 2010.

CHAPTER 4

[1]Reeve, Christopher. "Christopher Reeve's Decision" *Reader's Digest*, July, 1998, p. 60-66.

CHAPTER 6

[1]"Ask Arnold" *Shwarzenegger.com* n.d. Web 26 April 2010.
[2]Ross, Dena. "George Forman's Secound Chance" *Beliefnet.com* n.d. Web. 26 April 2010.

CHAPTER 7

[1]Amos, Wally. *The Famous Amos Story: The Face That Launched a Thousand Chips.* Doubleday, 1983.

CHAPTER 8

[1]Cater, Amanda. "If a Child" *Poemhunter.com* n.d. Web 27 April 2010.

CHAPTER 12

[1]Sherman, Elizabeth. "Confidence Is the Sexiest Thing a Woman Can Have." *Parade, Dallas Morning News Magazine,* June 21,1998. pp. 11-12.

PRAYER OF SALVATION

God loves you—no matter who you are, no matter what your past. God loves you so much that He gave His one and only begotten Son for you. The Bible tells us that "...whoever believes in him shall not perish but have eternal life" (John 3:16 NIV). Jesus laid down His life and rose again so that we could spend eternity with Him in heaven and experience His absolute best on earth. If you would like to receive Jesus into your life, say the following prayer out loud and mean it from your heart.

Heavenly Father, I come to You admitting that I am a sinner. Right now, I choose to turn away from sin, and I ask You to cleanse me of all unrighteousness. I believe that Your Son, Jesus, died on the cross to take away my sins. I also believe that He rose again from the dead so that I might be forgiven of my sins and made righteous through faith in Him. I call upon the name of Jesus Christ to be the Savior and Lord of my life. Jesus, I choose to follow You and ask that You fill me with the power of the Holy Spirit. I declare that right now I am a child of God. I am free from sin and full of the righteousness of God. I am saved in Jesus' name. Amen.

If you prayed this prayer to receive Jesus Christ as your Savior for the first time, please contact us on the Web at **www.harrisonhouse.com** to receive a free book.

Or you may write to us at

Harrison House • P.O. Box 35035 • Tulsa, Oklahoma 74153

The Harrison House Vision

Proclaiming the truth and the power

Of the Gospel of Jesus Christ

With excellence;

Challenging Christians to

Live victoriously,

Grow spiritually,

Know God intimately.

Fast. Easy. Convenient.

For the latest Harrison House product information and author news, look no further than your computer. All the details on our powerful, life-changing products are just a click away. New releases, E-mail subscriptions, testimonies, monthly specials—find it all in one place. Visit harrisonhouse.com today!

harrisonhouse

We Would Like to Hear From You

If you have prayed the salvation prayer for the first time, or if you have a testimony to share after reading this book, please contact us through our website at www.harrisonhouse.com.

Or you may write to us at:

Harrison House Publishers
P.O. Box 35035
Tulsa, Oklahoma 745153

www.harrisonhouse.com